Table of Con

D0112679

Lifting Up Jesus (in every talk) as We Proclaim His Gospel

"For I determined to know nothing among you except Jesus Christ and Him crucified."
— **The Apostle Paul** (I Corinthians 2:2)

A guide for Young Life Leaders (and others, too)

INTRODUCTION

Why such focus on Jesus?

1. **Perhaps, the biggest reason we share Jesus in every message, is that Jesus reveals the heart of God.**

   "No one has ever seen God, at any time, but the one and only Son, who is Himself God and is in closest relationship with the Father (is in the very bosom of the Father), has made Him known (has explained him)" **(John 1:18)**.

We'd only know God as almighty, omni — everything, infinite creator of the universe, if it wasn't for Jesus showing us God's heart. We are asking kids to trust the thing most precious to them, their very own hearts, to God. No one trusts anyone unless they are assured that the person is trustworthy, has a good heart, and truly cares for them. How would we know those things about God, if Jesus didn't show us God's heart? Often kids' hearts have been wounded because they trusted someone before and were hurt. This makes them even more reluctant to trust their hearts to God. In addition, they cannot "see" God. Jesus shows them God; Jesus makes God seeable, touchable, knowable, and trustable.

2. **When you lift up Jesus, (not religion or a case for Christianity) all people will be drawn to Him.**

   "Just as Moses lifted up the snake in the wilderness, so the Son of Man must be lifted up" **(John 3:14)**.

   "So Jesus said, 'When you have lifted up the Son of Man, then you will know that I am He ... '" **(John 8:28)**.

   "'And I, when I am lifted up from the earth, will draw all people to myself'" **(John 12:32)**.

George Sheffer (one of the first staff in Young Life) said: "If kids knew how wonderful the Savior is, they'd fall in love with Him."

Phillip Yancey tells the story of a Harvard professor, who when he heard someone say, "I don't believe in Jesus," would answer, "Tell me about this Jesus you don't believe in, because I probably don't believe in him either." Generally, people don't disbelieve in Jesus; rather, they have a distorted, warped view of Him. We have the opportunity to present the real Jesus.

3. **Forgiveness of sin (which is our greatest need) and union with God (which is our greatest hope) are found in Jesus.**

   "Salvation is found in no one else, for there is no other name under heaven given to people by which we must be saved" **(Acts 4:12)**.

   "But He was pierced for our transgressions, He was crushed for our iniquities; the punishment that brought us peace was on Him, and by His wounds we are healed. We all, like sheep, have gone astray, each of us has turned to our own way; and the Lord has laid on Him the iniquity of us all" **(Isaiah 53:5-6)**.

   "God made Him who had no sin to be sin for us, so that in Him we might become the righteousness of God" **(II Corinthians 5:21)**.

4. **Jesus is the best of Christianity — the best we have to present.**

   I heard of an experiment done on the Boulder campus of the University of Colorado. They filmed interviews with students randomly stopped on campus with this question: "We're doing a survey about where college students stand on religion in America. What do you think about Christianity?" The first fifty students responded negatively. It was unanimous. Fifty for fifty. They cited arrogance, intolerance, the Crusades, discrimination, the failing church, a sordid history, hypocrites, and more. Then, with the same introduction, they changed the question to: "What do you think about Jesus?" The next fifty students answered positively. No lie. Fifty for fifty. With great respect, they reflected on His character (laying down His life, standing up for what He believed in), His teaching, how He radically treated people equally, how He stood up to corrupt authority, and more.

   Ask anyone, "What is Christianity?" and he or she will most likely respond with things to believe in plus morals to live by. We simply lift up Jesus and a friendship with Him. Doctrines to believe, and a way to live, flow out of friendship with Jesus.

5. **Jesus truly knows our pain and our situations; He enters in and actually bears it with us.**

   "Because He Himself suffered when He was tempted, He is able to help those who are being tempted" **(Hebrews 2:18)**.

   "For we do not have a high priest who is unable to empathize with our weaknesses, rather we have one who has experienced all of life, just as we have … " **(Hebrews 4:15-16)**.

Lifting Up Jesus

As our creator, He made us. As the One who upholds the universe, He knows all about us. As the Incarnate One, He "gets" us. He identified with us, so that we can identify with Him.

Psalm 139:1-6 • Matthew 10:29-31.

6. *Jesus is Who we invite into our hearts.*
   People want and need to know Who is going to be living within them.

   "So that Christ may dwell in your hearts through faith" **(Ephesians 3:17)**.
   "God has chosen to make known among the Gentiles the glorious riches of this mystery, which is Christ in you the hope of glory" **(Colossians 1:27)**.

7. *Jesus lived life to the FULL, and He will impart that abundant life to us (from the inside out).*

   "I have come that they may have life, and have it to the full" **(John 10:10b)**.
   "For in Him we live and move and have our being" **(Acts 17:28)**.
   "'The Spirit of the Lord is on me, because He has anointed me to proclaim good news to the poor. He has sent me to proclaim freedom for the prisoners and recovery of sight for the blind, to set the oppressed free, [to heal the broken hearted from Isaiah 61] and to proclaim the year of the Lord's favor.' He began by saying to them, 'Today this scripture is fulfilled in your hearing'" **(Luke 4:17-21)**.

8. *Jesus is not only the One we trust with our lives, but we are also growing into His very image.*

   "For those God foreknew He also predestined to be conformed to the image of His Son ... " **(Romans 8:29)**.
   "And we all, who with unveiled faces contemplated the Lord's glory, are being transformed into His image with ever-increasing glory, which comes from the Lord, who is the Spirit" **(II Corinthians 3:18)**.
   People want to hear about the One they are becoming like.

9. *In a way I cannot explain, but we have all felt and experienced, when you speak the name "Jesus," there's a power and a presence in the room.*

   "Therefore God exalted Him to the highest place and gave Him the name that is above every name, that at the name of Jesus every knee should bow, in heaven and on earth and under the earth, and every tongue acknowledge that Jesus Christ is the Lord, to the glory of God the Father" **(Philippians 2:9-11)**.

10. **No one will ever love you like Jesus, and no one will ever be a friend to you like Jesus.**

   "Greater love has no one than this: to lay down one's life for one's friends"
   (John 15:13).

11. **One major difference between Christianity and all the other world religions is Jesus Christ.** None of them has a Savior. None speak of a God who comes to them. All other world religions are about our effort to get to god (not really our God even). None offer a remedy for sin. What they do offer is religious acts (works), traditions, and beliefs that if performed well move you closer to their god. We offer Jesus and a relationship with Him (accepting His death on our behalf to remove sin and taking Him as Lord), which opens up intimacy with God to us.

It is wise to memorize the five great Christological passages of Scripture.
Isaiah 53:1-6 • John 1:1-18 • Philippians 2:6-11
Colossians 1:15-22 • Hebrews 1:1-4

1. Your own heart will be encouraged and enlivened.

2. You will often draw on and use a phrase from these Scriptures as you speak of Jesus; such as, "He who actually bears our sorrows, and carries our griefs" (from Isaiah); or, "He who is in the very bosom of the Father, has explained Him" (from John); or He who "upholds the universe by the power of His Word" (from Hebrews), and more.

As you speak of Jesus, include the incarnation and its meaning in every talk.
"Jesus is the visible expression of the invisible God" (Colossians 1:15).
Jesus speaking, "He who has seen me has seen the Father"
(John 14:9).

1. Every person wants to know what God is really like …

   What does He feel? What does He think? What does He want from us? What does He think of me?

   We know what God is like by looking at Jesus.

2. "Does God care?" is answered in Jesus. Jesus' compassion and His heart's motivation to help people's needs, screams that God cares. Of course, Jesus giving His very life for our sake is the ultimate act of caring and friendship.

3. Does God know me, really? By God becoming a human in Jesus, "He has experienced all of life as we have, yet without sin" (Hebrews 4:15); and then, He even experienced sin (by becoming sin) on the cross. So, there is not one thing in our life Jesus cannot identify with — He knows it all.

4. Of course, Jesus "acts" like God would act — healing diseases, expelling demons, raising the dead, teaching with authority, creating something from nothing (food for 5,000), demonstrating incredible wisdom (as He answered all questions and entrapments), caring for all equally regardless of their earthly positions, knowing people's thoughts and their hurts, restoring people's dignity, standing up for the oppressed, being incredibly humble, showing anger at things that hindered people coming to God, and much more.

The big "how" to bring Jesus to life, in making Him real and relevant, is ...

1. You must live ("abide," John 8:31) in the Gospel event yourself until it is alive and vivid to you, unfolding before your very eyes. You can see it, hear it, feel it, smell it, see the look on people's faces, know what are people thinking, every detail. This will involve using your "divinely informed imagination" helping you picture the event. Have fun with this. Then, in your "talk," paint the picture of the event. Invite people into it with you. Jesus will come alive for them if we do this well.

2. Include in your talk the way that you have experienced Jesus in your life as it relates to sharing this event. Your proclamation is not outside of yourself; rather, you are connected to it. The "testimony" you give is not long, nor bringing too much self-attention — though it should be personal and appropriately vulnerable. Your testimony enhances and highlights Jesus' reality in our lives today (not just 2,000 years ago).

A Few Clarifying Words from the Author

1. Holding Jesus central and primary in every talk does not mean we are not "Trinity"-believing people. Of course, God is Father, Son, and Holy Spirit. It is interesting that the Father gave us His Son, and the Son gives us (brings us to) the Father. And, Jesus' first resurrected act was to give us His Spirit (John 20:21-22).

2. When using the expression "the talk," we mean an evangelistic message which opens up an aspect of Jesus as He connects with our "need" in our pursuit of abundant life and in our consideration of living life with Him.

3. Each talk does not necessarily include a full explanation of Jesus' dying on the cross (what it means), His rising, and His offer of life to the full with Him (and all about kingdom living). Rather, a good talk creates intrigue and a drawing to life with Jesus, as kids consider their own lives, and their views of God up to that point.

4. The hope of this book is to help stir up Jesus in you as you create each

talk you will present. This book provides some historical context, along with a few thoughts to help you build the "setting." It is oriented toward "outreach" talks, rather than Campaigners-type lessons.

5. What you know of kids, their culture, their questions, their life situations, their hopes and dreams, and their distorted views of God will always shape your talk. That's good.

6. This book highlights many possible "points" you could draw out of Jesus' miracles, words, and encounters. Obviously, you would not make all the points in any one talk. Choose one or two as the Spirit leads and the talk emerges. Of course, there are more points you can draw from a Jesus event than the ones presented here. You will have your own points. That's good.

Jesus' Encounter with Zaccheus

Found only in Luke 19:1-10

Background

1. When the Romans ruled a conquered land and its people, they allowed them to keep their "culture" as long as they acknowledged the Caesar as king (later, as god, too) and sent tax money to Rome. The Romans would make one of the conquered people (in this case, from the Jews of Israel) the "tax collector." There were no W-2 or 1040 income tax forms. Instead of H&R Block or tax attorneys to determine your fair share of taxes to pay, the tax collector would knock on your door with the full backing of the Roman army and demand tax money. Then, he would send enough money to Rome to satisfy them, and keep the rest for himself. So, the tax collector betrayed his nation (was considered a traitor), because he joined with the Romans and became rich off his own people. Needless to say, the tax collector was hated, ostracized, and disowned. The Jewish Mishnah said that tax collectors were so loathsome that they should not be considered as people.

2. The sycamore fig tree was the leafiest tree in Israel. There's a good possibility that you could not see Zaccheus in the tree that day. The Scripture never says "Jesus saw Zaccheus" in the tree, but that "Jesus looked up" from the road and called out his name. Picture Zaccheus looking through the leaves to see Jesus.

3. Meal sharing in the Jewish culture still today is **THE SIGN** of friendship. Everyone present that day clearly heard Jesus essentially say to Zaccheus, "Come down; I want to be your friend."

4. Also, in the Jewish culture, you didn't mix the clean with the unclean. A good Jew, trying to keep the law and live righteously for God, would not associate with a known sinner. Not only would it "bring you down" to a lower level, but it would contaminate you and therefore affect your status with God. Eating with Zaccheus might be akin to Billy Graham sharing a meal (accepting the invitation) at the home of the head of a mafia family (or the head of a drug cartel).

Setting the Scene

It was a parade. Folks began lining the streets — five, six or seven people deep — to see Jesus' procession pass by. What happens when you arrive at a parade and folks already have their position? Either you try to move up front and sit down (Zaccheus was hated and folks, of course, would not yield a good seat to him), or you try to see from the back (Zaccheus could not take a rear position because he was short). So, he climbed a tree.

Points You Could Make

1. Luke 19:1 — Jesus, the fullness of God dwelling in Him, did not expect people to come to Him … He didn't just teach in the synagogue. He again was out with people, in their towns, on their streets, in their fields and homes. God pursues us (Thomas Kelly calls Jesus "The Hound of Heaven"); it's not about us getting to God but God gently, relentlessly, finding us. God doesn't come to us only if we deserve it (Zaccheus certainly didn't deserve it), but because He wants a friendship. Bette Midler was wrong when she sang, "God is watching us … from a distance" (song of the year in 1993). He comes near to us.

2a. Luke 19:2 — The name Zaccheus means "The Righteous One." I can see his parents coming to the temple on the eighth day of Zaccheus' life to give thanks to God for giving them a son, having him circumcised, and dedicating him back to God naming him "The Righteous One." How did he go so far astray — making the choice to betray his people, his nation, his God? He "got" lost the same way we all "get" lost — one choice at a time. It's like how cows get lost in Texas. They just eat grass. They eat one clump of grass, then move to another, then another, then another, and two hours later they look up and say, "Where the heck is the herd?" They are lost, and they cannot get back to the herd on their own. They were just hungry and doing what they were made to do — eat grass. The same is true for Zaccheus — and us. We just want abundant, whole life — to be happy; so we make this choice in the hope that it will bring us life, then this choice, then this choice. We aren't scum, or gross, or evil. We're just doing what we are made to do — pursue life and happiness. Maybe he thought money would be good and bring life or power, or maybe he was "saving his skin" by winning favor with the powers that be. Who knows? He's just totally lost. He can't hit "re-deal" and start all over. He doesn't like being hated; he probably hates himself, feeling extreme shame. What hope does he have to change himself or his circumstances? None, on his own. You could possibly share some part of your own experience with being "lost."

2b. Imagine how Zaccheus feels (given #1 in background). He's alienated from his family, his friends, and his religion/God. He doesn't belong in his community; he's shunned and rejected. He's feeling shame and guilt. God must be disappointed and he probably hates himself. Help kids identify what they feel in common with Zaccheus. They deal with many of these same feelings.

3. Luke 19:3a — But he still (again like every human being) "wanted to see who Jesus was." No matter how far astray someone has gone from God, they still want to see God. That's because we are made in God's image (Genesis 1:27), and God has put "eternity into every person's heart" (Ecclesiastes 3:11). We all have a soul and a deep desire (or longing) to know God and be accepted by Him.

Verse 3b — Zaccheus had to persist, sacrifice, and risk to have a good look at Jesus. He could have given up, not been open, and not kept trying. This well-dressed man climbed a tree. He must have been laughed at. Also, Jesus didn't evaluate Zaccheus' motives for seeing Him; Jesus is only thrilled that he'd come to see Him. Same with us.

4. Luke 19:5 — Jesus calls Zaccheus by name. He's never met Zaccheus, He just knew him. Of course, the One of Whom it's said that all things have been created by Him and for Him, knew Zaccheus (Colossians 1:16). He once said, "Before I formed you in your mother's womb, I knew you" (Jeremiah 1:5). See also Psalms 139:7-10. We can present an image and fool others about who we really are; and we can hide (have secrets) from others about what we have done; but we can't fool God or hide anything from Him. God knows all about us — the good, the bad, and the ugly. That's either the most frightening thought we've ever had because we think that God will judge us and reject us; or, it's the most freeing thought we could ever have because God knows everything about us and is not disappointed in us and does not reject us. He still pursues us and invites us to be in a relationship with Him. We don't have to put on a certain face for God; He accepts us **just as we are**.

   Jesus didn't "call Zaccheus out" in front of the crowd saying, "Look everyone, there's a guy who has completely messed up … he's a traitor … a weasel … don't associate with him; don't be like him." We cannot hear the tone of Jesus' voice when He calls out Zaccheus' name (nor see Jesus' eyes), but my guess is that there was tenderness and love in His voice — not condemning, not shaming, not degrading. In fact, nowhere in the Gospels does Jesus condemn a pagan — only the rigid, religious people.

5. Luke 19:5 — "The Price is Right" stole the line from Jesus, "Come on down!" "Come" is one of Jesus' favorite words. (Matthew 11:28-30; John 7:37) It's an invitation. Jesus never takes away our choice; He respects us too much. He does not command Zaccheus to "get down" out of the tree. He does not compel him. He kindly invites him. Zaccheus could have refused to come down. He could have said, "I have an appointment at 2:30 p.m. … maybe tomorrow," or "My wife doesn't like me to bring a guest home unannounced," or "Naw, it just doesn't work for me." What do you think Zaccheus felt as he considered this invitation? Numb, overwhelmed, excited but afraid/fearful, skeptical and guarded. We feel all those same emotions when we realize God draws close to us.

6. Luke 19:5 — "I must be a guest at your home today." What does God want from us? How does God want to relate to us and us to Him? Our obedience, our worship and adoration should grow from "our friendship with God." He wants to be our friend, just like He came to the garden and shared life with Adam and Eve (Genesis 3:8).

7. Luke 19:6 — He "received Jesus gladly." Those are great words describing our coming to God. We just receive — not perform in order to gain favor, not achieve good standing, not get our act together, so we can then "get" God. We just receive Him. And, with joy — not out of duty, not begrudgingly, not with great resignation, but gladly. Paul Tillich said becoming a Christian is just "accepting God's acceptance of us."

8. Luke 19:7 — The crowd grumbled (or murmured) saying, "He's gone to be the guest of a known sinner." Doesn't this blow out of the water what you've thought about God up until now? What does this show us about God's heart? Does He shun us when we make bad choices in our pursuit of life? Does he agree with the world when they put us down? NO, the One who "upholds the universe by the power of His Word" pursues us, invites us near, and wants to be our friend. Jesus befriends us sinners.

9. Luke 19:8-9 — Zaccheus declares he'll give back all the riches he's obtained by cheating people in tax collecting. His repentance (literally making a 180-degree turn — from moving away from God or ignoring Him to seeking God and His way) is dramatic. But, it does not precede his friendship with Jesus. His repentance isn't "in order to" have the forgiveness and relationship with Jesus. It is "because of"; it grows out of his friendship with Jesus.

10. Luke 19:10 — "The Son of Man came to seek and to save the lost." Jesus shares one of His reasons that He came to earth. He wants every person to have the chance to know who God really is and how He feels about His image-bearers. You could weave in part of your personal story here — how you were lost and how Jesus pursued you.

11. Luke 19:9 — "Salvation has come to this house today … ." Salvation is a big word, but Jesus is essentially saying, "Zaccheus and I are now in relationship. We're friends. His sin — his past — is removed from him; behold, the new has come. He's on the way to knowing abundant life, wholeness, and all My Spirit has to offer." Zaccheus moved from an acquaintance with Jesus as teacher/historical figure to a life-changing encounter with Jesus as a friend/life-giver/redeemer. So can we.

A Leper Healed

Matthew 8:2-4; Mark 1:40-44;
Luke 5:12-14

Background

1. Leprosy is a slowly progressing disease of the nervous system, which used to be fatal. It was thought to be highly contagious and contracted by contact

with a person who had leprosy. As nerve endings died, first in the extremities (fingers, toes, neck, and head), great, oozing sores developed, which were accompanied by a horrible stench. Once it was known that someone had leprosy, the culture and the law in Jesus' day demanded that the sick person live quarantined from contact with any person including family; so, leper colonies formed outside the cities, where lepers lived until they died. If they did venture out from the colony, they had to scream out over and over, "unclean," so that people would clear away from the diseased leper.

2. To make matters worse, the accepted, dominant thought surrounding disease was that the person had sinned in some way, and therefore, was reaping his or her just reward from God ... to have leprosy meant that you had offended God and He was simply giving you what you deserved. In addition, the Jewish culture had certain conditions that made you "unclean," things like a woman's menstrual cycle (because of the blood), touching a dead body, or a skin disease or rash like leprosy among other things. When you were unclean, you could not go to the temple or synagogue and worship. You were considered not in communion (right-standing) with God.

Setting

Pretty straight forward ... Jesus is traveling from city to city, proclaiming His kingdom of living connected with God, healing every disease, and casting out demons. A leper approaches Him, certainly crying out in a loud voice, "unclean, unclean," with folks clearing away from him so as not to get too close and contract the disease, or to be "unclean" themselves in God's eyes (according to the teaching of that day).

Points You Could Make:

1. Mark 1:40 — The leper "fell on his knees, begging Jesus" ... What must this man (Jesus) have been like to move you to bow down to Him? Everyone who came to Jesus bowed down — from Jairus, the synagogue president (Mark 5:22), to this leper, to Satan himself (Luke 8:28). Have you ever been moved to bow down before another person?

2. Mark 1:40 — The leper says, "If you are willing ... ." What does this beginning phrase suggest?

   a. He recognizes that Jesus could do it — had the power to make this happen.

   b. But, it also suggests that the leper is wondering what motivates Jesus to do a miracle for someone, and/or the leper isn't sure what Jesus thinks about him ... how Jesus views Him (every kid wonders this, too). This miracle (and others) shows that God's heart is turned toward those hurting and in need, and He wants to engage and help. He does not turn away when we call out to Him. We know nothing about the leper's character or how well he's lived his life, honoring God or dishonoring God. Maybe he's lived a bad life and is a bad guy. If you've ever wondered, "What does God think of me?" Your answer is in the next verse.

    c.   How must the leper have felt? Help kids identify with the leper as they feel many of the same things: lonely, full of despair, angry/bitter, angry at God for what's happened, depressed, can't change circumstances, helpless and hopeless, and more.

3.   Mark 1:40 — The leper says, "you could make me clean." I wonder why he didn't say, "you could **heal** me?" Maybe it's because the leper knew he was dying (Dr. Luke says he was "a mass of leprosy" [Luke 5:12]); he was probably in an advanced stage of the disease, closing in on death. And, the leper didn't want to die not connected to God, as his "unclean" status told him he was. None of us wants to die disconnected with God. Maybe he was just asking to please be put in right standing with God before he died.

4.   Mark 1:41 — Jesus, "moved with compassion" … Here's how Jesus views us; here's how God's heart thinks of us and acts. The Greek word here is "*sphlochna*," for which we don't have a good English transaction. It means a person enters in and actually bears with whatever another person is going through. You actually "take on" the same "suffering" the person is suffering. So, we translate "*sphlochna*" with phrases like, "took pity on him", or "His heart went out to him," or "moved with compassion," or simply "loved him." We cannot look a kid in the eye and honestly say, "I was in high school (middle school), so I know what you're experiencing." The truth is, we don't know all a kid is going through. But, we can look a kid in the eye and say, "I know Someone who does know everything you're going through. His name is Jesus." The Scripture says, "We do not have a high priest (Jesus) who cannot sympathize with us in our weakness, but rather we have One who has experienced all of life as we have" (Hebrews 4:15; also Hebrews 2:18). Jesus "*sphlochnas*" us, as he "*sphlochnas*" the leper.

5.   Mark 1:41 — " … He stretched out His hand and touched the leper … ." Jesus could have simply said, "Leprosy be gone," and it would have been gone; but, He touched the leper. Why? How long had it been since the leper had been touched? (Remember, he was a "mass of leprosy.") Maybe a couple of years? UCLA did a study once and determined that a human being needs eight to 10 touches a day to be emotionally healthy. This was a double or triple miracle. Not only was the leprosy healed and the man was made clean (verse 44: the leper was to show himself to the priest to prove that his disease was gone and he was now "clean" in God's eyes), but his emotional self, which was greatly wounded through the leprosy, was restored to health because Jesus touched him. Jesus knowing us thoroughly, including our insides too, wants our whole self to be made whole, complete,

healthy. This may be the most beautiful part of the miracle — the touch. NOTE: Jesus touches the leper while he's in his "unclean" leprous condition, then He heals him. Again, Jesus (God) enters in, and bears our condition, with us.

6. Mark 1:41 — Jesus said, "I am willing ... ." Of course, Jesus is willing. He loves us and wants the best for us. His heart is drawn to us. He enters in and "takes on" all our "stuff," our situation. Always know, at all times, that **Jesus is willing,** or He ceases to be Jesus. He is not reluctant to help us. He does not hold back. Don't let your feelings of unworthiness stop you from receiving Jesus' touch, because your feelings of unworthiness do not deter Jesus from coming to you. Jesus willingly enters into all our mess, brokenness, failures, bad choices, pain and hurt.

7. Mark 1:42 — "Immediately the leprosy left him, and he was cleansed." You could imagine how this former leper felt. Try to describe it. How do you feel knowing you are cleansed and whole, which is what we call "salvation"? (For an explanation of salvation see #1, Point 11.) How do you feel when Jesus willingly enters into your mess and pain?

The Reasons Jesus Came to Earth, as Given by Jesus Himself

Luke 19:10; Mark 10:45
"I have come that they may have life, and have it to the full" **(John 10:10b).**

Jesus spoke three times, "I have come ... ." He gives the purpose statements for His life, His *"raison d'etre"* (His reason for being). The first two are self-explanatory, yet very profound. Jesus is seeking to save the lost (Luke 19) and is giving His very life so we can be forgiven and connected to God (Mark 10). Wow! It's the John passage that we'll expand on here.

In John 10:10b, Jesus says, "I have come to give life, and life abundantly."

    a. The Greek word life is *"zoë,"* which means the life that comes from God ... the life God gives ... the life God creates ... the life He wants to impart with depth and great quality.

    b. The Greek word abundantly is *"perosis,"* which means as you pour water into a cup, it becomes full, but you keep on pouring as it overflows onto the floor. More water than you need — continually coming, never stopping.

Jesus only knows how to give abundantly. Think of the best wine at the wedding in Cana (John 2), or the 12 baskets of leftovers after the feeding of the 5,000 (Matthew 14), or the greatest catch of fish so that nets were breaking (Luke 5). How would you define abundant life? What is abundant life to you (to your audience)? Is it the circumstances lining up in life as you wish … great friends, being an all-star player, parents who get along, good grades, good health, and no bad or hard things coming your way? Or is it "inner things" like joy, being authentic, having character, purpose and meaning, liking yourself, fulfillment, peace, being a better friend/caring for others more selflessly, handling with strength difficult situations that happen to you, being wise, or something else?

Not that Jesus doesn't care about the circumstances of our lives (He does), but Jesus' offer of abundant life (perosis zoë) leans toward the "inner things." Jesus' inaugural address, introducing Himself and His three years of ministry, is recorded in Luke 4:14-22 (quoting Isaiah 61:1-2), which was prophecy years ago about the Messiah [Jesus] who would come:

> The Spirit of the Sovereign LORD is on me, because the LORD has anointed me to proclaim good news to the poor. He has sent me to bind up the brokenhearted, to proclaim freedom for the captives and release from darkness for the prisoners, to bring recovery of sight for the blind, to proclaim the year of the LORD's favor and the day of vengeance of our God, to comfort all who mourn (Isaiah 61:1-2).

This is a fuller explanation of the abundant life Jesus wants to impart to us, which He wants to help us grow into and experience.

"To proclaim good news to the poor"

The poor here means those actually living in poverty (economic, and all the accompanying issues with being poor) and/or, those "poor in spirit," the spiritually poor (those who aren't close to God). The Good News is that God loves the poor dearly, and it's never too late to draw near to Him and experience healing, wholeness, and everything listed below in living life with Jesus. Mother Theresa always said that the worst poverty humans experience is loneliness.

"Recovery of sight for the blind"

Surely this means more than literal blindness. The world programs us to bias, to prejudice, to categorize people according to the world's standards, and we need fresh eyes — a new lens to view situations and people through God's eyes.

"To heal the brokenhearted"

Most everyone has experienced some wound to their hearts from a betrayal, a death, or a horrible life circumstance. John Eldredge says, "Every person has a Father Wound," meaning that in some way this most influential person in our lives has injured our hearts. (Even the best fathers are human.) Counselors can help us identify and name these hurts, but God offers healing.

"Release from what oppresses us"

Often, worry, anxiety, depression (of all levels), even jealousy and bitterness can weigh us down, and affect our thinking and how we live. They can rob us of joy. Satan's lies like, "I don't matter. I am alone. I don't have what it takes to make it in this world. I am not worthy to have anyone love me," can get into our spirit and mind as if they are the truth. We need to be released to enjoy God, ourselves and life.

"Freedom from what holds us captive or as a prisoner"

So much can control us. Things like anger or fear. Things like shame and guilt. We might be driven by a sport or a person to succeed or to act in a way contrary to who we really are. We desire freedom. As Kirkegaard (the great Danish philosopher) said when he began his relationship with Jesus, "Now Lord, with your help, may my true self emerge." That's freedom.

Give examples of how things mentioned here were part (or are a part) of your own life, and how Jesus has entered in and helped you experience abundant life. You probably haven't "arrived" yet — like what needed healing is all healed now, or you are completely free of _____. However, that thing that controlled you or influenced you no longer has the same place in your life. It may rear its head, so to speak, but it doesn't have the control it used to, as you and Jesus go on together.

 # Man by the Pool 38 Years – Made Well

Found only in John 5:1-9

Background

1. In Jesus' day, there was no accommodation for the disabled or handicapped ... no special parking places, ramps, electric wheelchairs, braille in the elevators, nothing. If you were disabled, you all were gathered together, mostly to beg, even for your food. Often, those begging would find strategic places, like at the city gate or at the entrance to the temple, where many people would pass by. However, this event indicates they also gathered around the Pool of Bethsaida in Jerusalem. Why there? It was thought that when God stirred the waters of the pool, the first one into the water was healed. This seems ludicrous at first glance because if you're paralyzed, how do you get to the pool at all? And, how many could actually gather by the edge of the pool for the best chance of being the first one

in. Even with all the historical research available today, we're not certain if there actually were times the water stirred and someone was healed, but we do know that this was the prevailing thought and that there was quite a collection of blind, paralyzed, lame, and sick persons gathered at this pool. How many? We can't know for sure, but it says a multitude.

2. The Israelite people, the Hebrew nation, had seven festivals during the year. These were feasts and celebrations, a time to cease work (often for a whole week) and remember God's provision and care for them. There was a Feast of Tabernacles (or Booths) remembering God's provision during their 40 years in the wilderness, where they lived in tents (booths). There was a feast celebrating God's provision in the harvest time (Feast of First Fruits). However, the biggest celebration was the Passover where the Jewish people remembered when they were slaves in Egypt and God had each Israelite family kill a lamb (a sacrifice) in their home and spread the blood around their doorpost. That night an angel of death killed the firstborn in every household in Egypt unless the blood of the sacrificed lamb was on the doorpost. The Egyptians, mourning their great loss of children, cried out to Pharaoh to release the Jewish slaves from their country, which he did. On Passover, every Jewish family tried to travel to Jerusalem, home of the temple (where God resided in the Holy of Holies), to celebrate. The city swelled in population by several hundred thousand, and it was said over 300,000 sheep (lambs) were sacrificed on Passover eve.

3. Jerusalem was a fortified city, completely surrounded by a wall. Still today, you can walk on top of the wall all the way around the city. There were five gates, by which one could pass in and out of the city. Each gate had a name and a purpose. One gate was designed for animals to enter the city, called the Sheep Gate. Imagine 300,000 lambs being paraded into the city to be sold for Passover meals. The sounds, the smell, the poop and stepping in it, as the herds came through the gate. Be assured, people didn't travel much to this part of the city. This is where the sick and the lame were allowed — by the pool, which was located at the Sheep Gate.

Setting

It is Passover Week, so the city is teeming with people. Literally, thousands of animals are coming through the Sheep Gate. The sun is out, heating up the smell of poop. The pool of Bethsaida is right there, with a multitude of lame and sick. I'm sure there are no port-a-potties, so that smell is in the air as well. The Scripture says there are five porticoes by the pool. These are structures (some historical research say giant, wide arches) with a roof, supported by columns. Visualize the sick scrambling and packed in, to be under the shade of the porticoes or to be by the water's edge of the pool. How is this multitude getting food? How must these people be feeling? This place must be

Lifting Up Jesus

depressing, full of despair with little hope, and no energy for life. Are wounds festering? Is there pain and moaning you can hear?

Points You Could Make

1. Jesus, the God of the universe, goes to this place of pain and despair. No one else goes there; they avoid the Pool of Bethsaida at all costs. What does it say about God's heart that He goes there? Maybe the disciples even wait outside, as it doesn't mention them with Jesus. Or, maybe, there wasn't room enough for them to walk in that crowd with Jesus. As He walks in among the sick, what is in Jesus' mind? He's hurting with these people; He's weeping; He's sad they are not enjoying this life He created. How do we know that? The Scripture tells us: Isaiah 53:4 —"Surely our griefs He bore, and our sorrows He carried"; and Hebrews 4:15-16 — "For we do not have a high priest (a term for Jesus) who cannot sympathize with our weakness/ suffering; but rather, we have One who has experienced all of life as we have." Jesus, revealing God's heart toward us, is compassionate, meaning "suffering with." He enters into our "stuff." He understands; He "gets us."

2. John 5:5-6 — Jesus knew this man — that he had been 38 years in his sickness. Though He had never met this man, He knew him because He dreamed him up, and knit him together in his mother's womb and birthed him, and watched over him every day of his life — JUST LIKE HE HAS US. There are nearly seven billion people on planet Earth, and God knows each one of us — all about us. And, He pursues us, relentlessly and tenderly, though never taking away our choice. Often, He comes to us and woos us or coaxes us to enter into His story for us. Share from your life how you've experienced God's entering into your life and inviting you into more.

3. John 5:6 — Jesus asks the man, "Do you want to get well?" That's either the "dumbest question ever" (as my kids say to me sometimes when I ask them a question), or it is the most profound question ever. The Greek word translated "well" is hygies (the root of which yields our English word hygiene). It means whole, complete, full, and healthy. It's a big word; it has depth and quality to it. (See #3 for a full description of the abundant life Jesus offers and came to give.)

   At first thought, we would answer, "Of course, I want to get well"; but, what if it means changing something in our lives we don't want to change? For example, I might say I want to lose ten pounds, but if that means giving up French fries, pasta, potato chips, and sweets, then I'm not so sure. If "getting well" means looking at my life, how I live, how I think (making decisions based on what's important to me), giving up control, or risking a new direction, then, "no thanks," I'll stay where I am. Give examples from your own life of the difficulties that changes bring in "getting well," particularly in orienting your life with Jesus. Jesus is about so much more than whether or not we will go to heaven or hell when we die. He is the inventor of life, and He wants to impart being "well" to us. Rose, the elderly woman telling her story in the movie "Titanic," said at the end of the movie about Jack (the Leonardo DiCaprio character), "I guess you could say he saved me in about every way a person could be saved." That captures Jesus helping us "get well."

4. John 5:7-9 — The man's answer is not enthusiastic, like he really believes in Jesus. He almost offers an excuse, "This is my life. These are the cards I've been dealt. This is who I am." It's the same for us. We have a hard time seeing life connected with God, where Jesus is a dear friend, guiding us and imparting life, being "well" and growing into more "well." This lack of seeing it, not being able to understand life with Jesus at first, doesn't deter Jesus. He still pursues us and offers abundant life. It led to a miracle for this man, and for us.

5. John 5:8-9 — The man became "well" and immediately picks up his pallet and walks. This is a miracle. Yes, we become "well" immediately when we accept Jesus, but changes don't all come instantly. We have to grow into our wellness; it's a lifelong process, as we are helped by Jesus, our constant companion. You could share something from your own life of growing into "well," guided and helped by Jesus.

Feeding the 5,000+
Matthew 14:13-34; Mark 6:32-44;
Luke 9:10-17; John 6:1-14

Background

1. This miracle is the only miracle of Jesus (other than the resurrection) that appears in all four Gospels. That alone makes it very significant.

2. The Sea of Galilee is more like an oval-shaped lake (four miles wide and 12 miles long), as you can easily see across it in any direction. So, the people watching the boats cross the lake and running around the lake to meet the boats is not a stretch.

3. The contours of the land around the lake allow for cliffs to the water's edge, as well as more meadow-type fields gently sloping down to the lake. A remote field setting, not near any city but still near the lake, exists even today near Capernaum.

4. Crowds were counted in Jesus' day by the number of men in attendance, so with women and children added, this miracle could have been, in actuality, "The Feeding of the 10,000."

The Setting

In Luke's account (Luke 9:1-11) Jesus sent out His apostles (the 12) for their first ministry experience on their own. As they were returning to report with great joy and enthusiasm all they had seen, said, and done, there was not time to discuss and process with Jesus because of the crowd's needs and desire to be near Jesus. So, with sunset approaching, the apostles wanted to send the crowd away (Luke 9:12).

Matthew and Mark set the scene a bit differently. Jesus has just heard of his cousin and forerunner — John the Baptist's horrific beheading at the whim of Herod. He's grieving the loss of a loved one, and certainly this heightens His focus on His own impending death. He wants to get away, so He and the disciples load up the boats and cross over to a "lonely place" along the shore (a no-city landing). But, the crowd sees them and follows them around the lake to meet them as they land. (Matthew 14:14; Mark 6:32-33).

Points You Could Make

1. Mark 6:34 — You are grieving the death of a loved one/family member, and have been selflessly giving yourself away for the good of others for some time now, and you want some down time for yourself and your close friends. Yet, you are bombarded, much like the paparazzi pursue (dare I say, harass) people, with more needs, more cries for help, no time alone. How would you react if you were Jesus? How you think Jesus reacts influences the way you view God and how He reacts to us — to our not catching on, to our constant needs, to our expectations of how He should fix our situations, and to our desperate cries for help. Jesus, God Himself on Earth, reveals His heart toward us. He has COMPASSION; that's His reaction. Does God get "tired" of all our stuff always before Him? No, He provides.

    This word "compassion" in verse 34 appears 12 times in the Gospels. It is the deepest Greek word for love. The root is "*sphlochna*," which means the bowels, or a person's deepest place. So, from God's (Jesus') deepest place, He loves us. The fullness of "*sphlochna*" is that you "enter in" and literally "take on" and "bear with" whatever it is the person is feeling and going through. You could possibly relate a time in your life when you sensed God bearing with you in a tough, hurtful, or weird situation.

2. Mark 4:34 — As Jesus knows everything about us, He uses the phrase as He views us (the crowd in this event), "they are like sheep without a shepherd." How are we like sheep? Sheep need to be shown where to go for good grass to eat and for good water to drink. Left on their own, they will stop and eat weeds that could kill them, and they would drink stagnant, rancid water, which could make them sick. Sheep cannot defend themselves from predators; they need protection. They will lay down in such a way to rest that they cannot right themselves and get up on their own (it's called

being "cast down"). If they don't come to the shepherd to be cared for with things like burrs being removed, insects/parasites plucked from their nose and eyes, and their coat being combed, they will look straggly and sickly, and they'll be lethargic and sedentary. Sheep are made for a good shepherd. Where do we look for life on our own? How are we doing on our own in trying to make life work (what are the weeds and stagnant water we eat and drink)? How do we "right ourselves" when we're cast down? Jesus' view of the crowd (and of us) is that they have no shepherd. It also seems kids follow bad shepherds, who lead them astray. Do you have a personal part of your story to share here?

3. Could this have really happened as it is told? Five loaves and two fish multiplied to feed 10,000 people? Couldn't it have been Jesus' great teaching on love and living in the kingdom of God that moved people to selfless sharing with each other; so that there was enough food to go around for all to eat and be satisfied? No, this miracle shows Jesus was God Himself on earth. Jesus, Who was in essence God, could create food for all. Dale Bruner once said, "Don't you love God's new math: 5+2=10,000 … He's God; He could do that easily." Jesus once said, *"If you do not believe me (that I am God), believe the works, that you may know and understand that the Father is in me, and I am in the Father" (John 10:38).*

And, it fit God's M-O (motis operandi … the way God does things). He is motivated by a need as if He has a need meter in His heart that goes off, and He meets that need. He doesn't show off or call attention to the fact that He's just performed one of the greatest miracles of all time; rather, He stays in the background while the disciples hand out the food. He does things in good order, having folks sit down in groups … there's not chaos or people pushing and shoving to get food like you see sometimes in news reports of food coming in relief to a famine-stricken area.

4. This would be considered an impossible or insurmountable situation — 10,000 people, desolate place, no food. What's the situation in your life with no solution you can see with human eyes? Our first reaction is usually to practically solve it or to do what we can, just like the disciples in Mark 6:36, "Send everyone away so that they may go into the surrounding countryside and buy themselves something to eat." Yes, that's **ONE** solution. But, are we trapped in our earthly paradigm? Would you turn to God? Often we might turn to God and tell Him how to fix it, and when He does not do what we say, and right away when we say, then we pin on God that He didn't come through for us. Consider John 6:6, "He (God) knew what He intended to do." Jesus is God and absolutely in control (or He's not God, is He?). He's not caught off guard or surprised by our situation. Notice when Jesus starts acting, He doesn't tell everyone, "Settle down. I'll get you some food. Just cooperate and do what I say." No, we take steps with God, not knowing how

things will turn out, trusting He's in control, and He's good, and He's got my/ our good in His mind. Do you have a personal story here?

5. Often we'll feel inadequate or small in the face of a situation way beyond us. What is a little boy's smashed bag lunch in the face of 10,000 hungry people? That's not the way God sees things. He doesn't see impossible, marginalized, battered, wounded, or ugly; rather, He sees things as how they can be if we let God touch them. He can take what we offer Him, what little mess we are, and He'll make it beautiful, whole, and together. What do you make of twelve basketfuls left over? (Mark 6:43) That's God. When He makes wine, it's vintage wine (John 2:10). When He goes fishing, He catches a boatload so the boats are sinking (Luke 5:7). When He makes food, it's 12 basketfuls left over. When Jesus gives life, it's abundantly (John 10:19b see #3 for full explanation of abundant life). That's the way God works. Imagine the little boy going home telling his mom about what happened with the lunch she made him … . Do you have a story from your life, how God took your mess and made it beautiful — way more than you expected?

6. How would you remember this miracle? What would you title it: "The day _____"? Of all the possible answers you might give, I wouldn't have thought of how the disciples referred to it: " … where they ate the bread after the Lord had given thanks" (John 6:23).

What impressed them was Jesus' gratitude over what they had, even though it was only a few loaves and fish. And, that is a great lesson in our pursuit of, and in our living of, life. We don't have to look hard to find many things for which we can be grateful that God has given us. This builds peace and can turn our hearts toward God and His wonderful provision.

7. The crowd was in a desolate place (Mark 6:35), also called a lonely place. Many of us find ourselves there as we live life. Do we turn to God, who wants to meet our needs in a desolate place? And often, God provides in ways we wouldn't have been able to predict. Do you have a personal God experience to tie in here?

The Great Catch of Fish and the Calling of Peter

Luke 5:1-11

This event is unique, recounted only in Luke. However, Matthew 4:18-22 and John 1:40-42 tell of Jesus' calling of Peter (formerly Simon), Andrew, James, and John to be disciples (later to be named apostles).

Background

Peter was a fisherman (most likely so was his father and grandfather. It was the family business.) The Sea of Galilee (see #5 Background to know more about the Sea of Galilee) is below sea level and is extremely plentiful with fish. Still today, fishermen go out in small vessels (much like Peter's boat), catch fish with nets, and sell them on the shore. You fish at night, because the sun's heat drives the fish deeper to cooler waters during the day; thus, no fish are near the surface to catch with nets. After the night's fishing, the rope of the nets might have torn, leaving a hole where fish could escape, so it would have to be mended. And, there might be seaweed and other "gunk" caught up in the nets that would need to be cleaned out.

Setting

Picture this scene in your mind's eye. The crowd is pressing in around Jesus to hear Him speaking by the Sea of Galilee. Jesus is being slowly pushed toward the water by the crowd. He gets into a boat (Peter's boat) and sits down (the accepted position of a rabbi when teaching) in the boat, and continues teaching with the crowd on the beach/shore line with water as a buffer between Him and the crowd.

Points You Could Make

1. Luke 5:1 — "The multitude was pressing in and listening to the word of God ... ."

    How many people are in a multitude? Other times the Scripture says "crowd," here, it says multitude. Have you ever been part of a crowd/mob/multitude where you couldn't really move, but as the crowd moved you were pushed along ... like at a concert or sporting event? That's what this must have been like — the multitude pressing in ... and why? To hear a man teach. What must it have been like to hear Jesus, God in the flesh, the Creator of the universe, talk about the life He created — how to live, how to view His Father, what His intentions are, how He wants to relate to us and us to Him? The Bible says (in Matthew 7:29 and other places, too) that the people were amazed (marveled) at His teaching ... that He taught as One with authority, not as their rabbis. There was a line from a drama production of Jesus's life called **Cotton Patch Gospel** describing the multitude's attraction to Jesus: "They drank every drop that dripped from the Savior's lips." How long do you think they stayed? Were they "fidgety"? Did they look at their watches? No, they were enthralled with Jesus. This doesn't fit our culture's view of Jesus, does it? Our culture holds Jesus at arm's length, or runs the other way when it comes to Jesus. Not so in His day. They couldn't get close enough to Him, or get enough of Him. He was magnetic; all kinds of people were attracted to Him. (Even though Isaiah 53:2 says that there was nothing in His physical appearance that we would be attracted to Him.)

2. Luke 5:2-4 — Everyone has formed impressions about Jesus. It's not like you haven't thought about Him before. Could those impressions be skewed/wrong/distorted? (Tell a story about how once in your life you formed an impression [of anyone or anything] that later turned out to be wrong.) How would you discover the real story about someone? The truth about someone? You investigate for yourself. You get close enough to find out what's real and what's not. Peter had heard things about Jesus no doubt. Word had spread like wildfire among the people as to miracles He performed and things He said. He'd read the papers and watched CNN. Now Peter was close enough to find out for himself. Give Jesus a chance to reveal to you His "real self" … get close enough/open enough to see for yourself.

3. Luke 5:4-5 — Jesus asked the absurd. Peter, a fisherman by trade, was asked by a teacher/carpenter (who happened to be God Himself, though Peter doesn't know that yet, but will know that in a moment) to go fishing in the middle of the day. Common knowledge accepted by everyone is that you don't fish in the middle of the day; the fish are down too deep in cooler waters. On top of this fact, they've already cleaned and mended their nets and are coming off a bad fishing night where they caught nothing. The fish just aren't "running" right now. Sometimes our thinking might go something like this: "I know my life because I'm living it after all. I have a strong idea what I need and what's right for me. What I sense God saying or asking me to do is to consider a friendship with Him. That seems contrary to common knowledge. Why would I do that? God's asking for my heart and wants to live there? Absurd." Note that Peter is never promised an outcome (a catch of fish) if he casts his net in deep water. God just says, "Go with me on this one." (You could share a time in your life that Jesus invited you into "deep water." There are all kinds of deep water: relational, personal, spiritual, directional in life, something that needs to change in your life.) Peter does "trust" the carpenter and does let down his nets. The reason he does is, "because you (Jesus) say so." He's not all-in on this deal. He's not telling all his buddies to watch what happens. He is reluctant and cautious. But, he is willing. And, that's OK. First steps with Jesus are usually very tentative. Reluctant trust is OK. Jesus doesn't say to Peter, "Well, forget it if you're not excited."

4. Luke 5:6-7 — They don't have a nice catch of fish or just the best catch of the year. No, they receive the best catch of their lives. Boats are sinking as they are filled with fish. In John 10:10b, Jesus says, "I have come to give life, and life abundantly." (To read a fuller reflection on what this abundant life is, refer to #3).

5. Luke 5:8-9 — What would your reaction be to this overwhelming miracle of catching more fish than you could ever imagine? Verse nine tells us "amazement had seized them." Of course, it had! Wouldn't there be

cheering, celebration, high fives? Maybe with some quick thinking, Peter would pull out a contract for Jesus to sign, locking him into a day of fishing just four times a year. How do you explain Peter's reaction? He falls at Jesus' knees (because the boat is full of fish, he can't get to Jesus' feet!) saying, "Depart from me, for I am a sinful man, O Lord." What is going on here?

a. Peter recognizes Jesus is God. All other false impressions he's had up until now are blown away. If you came face to face with God, what would you do? I'd wager we'd fall on our faces, too. When we see God for who He is, we also see ourselves, naked, our true selves, for who we really are. And, we'd see that we haven't lived our lives with the intent of honoring God, seeking God, enjoying God ... that we had fallen short. We'd recognize our "sin." What is sin? Sin is the attitude of our hearts where we essentially say (not in audible words, but in our spirit and actions) "Thanks for making me, God, in Your image, but I'll take it from here. I'll be the captain of my life, not You, God." And, we go our own way. The consequence of sin in our hearts are sins; that is, the things we do that dishonor God and hurt other people and ourselves. Peter, like us, feels/senses/knows that his "sin" (his heart's disposition) makes him guilty before God (even feels shame), and it alienates him from God. That is sin's effect (see Colossian 1:21-22; Romans 3:22-23; Romans 6:23; Ephesians 2:5; Isaiah 53:6). This is why Jesus died on the cross ... to bear our sin, and its effect, transferring to us His righteousness, making the way for us to be able to live life in perfect relationship with God (see 2 Corinthians 5:21).

b. Luke 5:10 — What is Jesus' reaction to Peter? Does He pounce on the moment to make sure Peter understands his sinfulness? Does He use this as a teachable moment so we know for sure more about the human condition? Does Jesus speak about of how offended He is at Peter's sin — how hurtful it has been to Him (see Genesis 6:5-6)? Does Jesus even acknowledge that Peter is correct in his assessment of himself? No, no, no, and no. Are we scum, or gross, or evil because sin rules our hearts? No, we are still God's image–bearers, beautifully and wonderfully made (Psalm 139:13-14). Is God disappointed in us and turns from us with disdain? No, Jesus' reaction to Peter is God's reaction to us. He says three things to Peter (combining with Jesus' words from the Matthew, Mark and John accounts of the calling of Peter.)

    i. "Do not fear" (or do not be afraid). Psychiatrists say that fear is the biggest influence on human's behavior. We run from fear. We control things around fear. We comply out of fear. God doesn't want us to cower from Him afraid, or comply to Him out of fear. He loves us, wants the best for us, has good intention toward us, and hopes we will choose to receive love and life from Him. His first words are, "Don't be afraid of me."

    ii. "Follow Me" — What do you attach yourself to in the hope that it will bring you life? What do you pursue, seek after, strive for, and

Lifting Up Jesus

give yourself to in the hope of the life you want? Jesus says, "Give yourself to Me" ... attach to Me. The term "follow Me" means "apprentice yourself to Me" ... learn from Me how to walk with Me and do LIFE.

iii. "I will make you" ... (in this case "a fisher of men"). Wow, this idea is that God has dreamed you up, knit you together in your mother's womb, birthed you, watched over you every day of your life, and longs to impart to you His *perosis zoë*. (See #3 for explanation). Let Him write the story of your life, rather than you controlling it. He has big plans for us. And, we just need to live into them. He wants to shape us into His person. His Spirit living in us brings the changes we desire. (See Philippians 1:6) You could share a story (or a part) of how "He's making you."

7 Jesus and Peter Walking on Water
Matthew 14:22-36; Mark 6:45-51; John 6:15-21

Background

1. Even though the Sea of Galilee is not large (four miles wide at its widest point and 12 miles long at its longest point and shaped like an oval), either a storm can come so quickly through the Valley by Arbela (from the east) or a great wind may simply arise, that a boat out on the sea cannot get to shore in time to avoid the turbulent waters. The body of water was/is not big enough for larger boats. Still today, the sea is fished with smaller vessels. In Jesus' day, motors for boats had not come into existence yet; however, these storms or winds can happen so quickly and be so violent that in 1988, even in the age of motors, six fishermen lost their lives on the Sea of Galilee because of raging waters swamping the boat before they could reach the shoreline.

2. So, in this event, the Scripture never says it was a "storm"; it only says "a strong wind was blowing" (John) or "the wind was dead against them" (Matthew and Mark). I once was visiting the Sea of Galilee and was awakened at night by a strong wind and went outside. Under a bright moon, I could see all the way to the other side of the sea, and the waves were huge, two or three feet high. Trying to visualize how the disciples in the boat could see Jesus walking on the water on a dark night and in a storm is difficult. Perhaps, it was a bad wind on a clear night, as it was the night of my visit.

3. In Bible days they referred to time in "watches" during the night, originating from a sentinel's military watch over the city. There were four watches during the night: sunset to 9 p.m., 9 p.m. to midnight, midnight to 3 a.m., and the fourth watch (in our event) was 3 a.m. to 6 a.m. (Matthew 14:25).

Setting

This event begins after a long day of Jesus' teaching, concluded by the feeding of the 5,000 (upwards to 10,000 in actuality). Jesus dismisses the crowd (how do you do that? Send 10,000 people home? That, in itself, is a miracle, and shows how people would listen to Him); and also, sends the disciples across the lake to Capernaum, saying He'll catch up.

Points You Could Make

1. Matthew 14:22 — "He (Jesus) **made** the disciples get into the boat, and go ahead of Him to the other side (of the Sea of Galilee) ... ." The disciples did exactly what Jesus told them to do.

   You've heard the expression, "in God's will"? The disciples were absolutely "in God's will". They were not outside of God's will, making a bad decision on their own; no, they were obedient to Jesus' command. However, something bad happened. A difficult circumstance of life came upon them. Following Jesus, being "in God's will," obeying God, does not guarantee that life will go the way you want it to go. We are not entitled to good things; nor do we earn or deserve an easy life by how well we live or do "godly" things. Bad things can happen for good people ... we live in a fallen world. The converse is true in experience too — good things can happen for bad people. There are 32,000 promises from God in the Bible, not one of them is: "Life will go perfectly fine for you if you give Me your heart and trust Me." God does promise that He will come to you in our hard times and walk with us, strengthening us and helping us get through it. And, He will use life circumstances to teach us and mold us into the person He desires us to be.

2. Matthew 14:25 — "Jesus came to them ... ." Jesus comes to us, especially in our times of trouble. (see Psalm 145:18) You could recall an example from your own life.

3. Matthew 14:25 — " ... walking on the water." You have to love Jesus' style as He comes to them, walking on the water. Of course, He could do that because He made the lake. Jesus will uniquely come to you, often when we least expect it (the disciples weren't even calling out for Him). Jesus may come to you in nature, or in a dream, or through something you read, or through another person, or through an inner knowing (some call this a "still, small voice" within you, or simply a nudge toward something). Possibly, share an example from your own life of how Jesus has come to you.

4. Matthew 14:26 — "the disciples were frightened, saying, "It's a ghost." We may not recognize Jesus when He comes to us at first, but He always reveals Himself. He wants to be known. (He is not a God in hiding or like a rabbit in front of the greyhounds they can never catch.) **"Immediately**, *Jesus spoke, "Take courage, it is I* [He identified Himself.]; *don't be afraid"* (Matthew 14:27). Neither does Jesus want us to be afraid of Him.

5. Matthew 14:28 — Peter answered, "Lord, if it's really you, tell me to come to you on the water." Some might see this as a bad or wrong prayer, kind of calling Jesus' bluff. First, the best prayer is the honest cry from our heart. And secondly, you might pray this kind of prayer someday, something like, "Lord, I don't know if you are real. I might be just talking into the air. But, if You are real, reveal Yourself to me in a way I can know it's You, and I will follow You." This is an OK prayer, but it must be sincere and honest; and, you must be willing to follow Jesus when He shows Himself to you.

6. Matthew 14:28 — Picture Peter getting out of the boat when Jesus says, "Come on then." (See #1 Zaccheus for discussion on Jesus saying, "Come.") Peter has his hands on the side of the boat lifting one leg over the side with his foot touching the water (to see if it will hold). The thoughts racing through his mind as he considers walking on water are a picture of us when we consider coming to Jesus at His invitation to begin a relationship.

    a. Peter wants to do it. It looks like the great adventure — better than rowing hard and bailing water out of the boat. He thinks he heard clearly from God, "Come," and his mind tells him God wouldn't call him to death or to less of life. But his friends (in the boat) are saying, "Don't do it Peter. Come on and row. We'll make it … this is crazy. You'll get messed up. You're alone on this one, Peter." Friends not joining with you is hard.

    b. Peter's afraid. He could sink and die, if the water doesn't hold. Yes, there is some fear in accepting Jesus. It's unknown to you. You haven't done it before. It takes trust — trusting what you know of Jesus so far and His offer of Life to you, and stepping out.

    c. Peter might say, "Could we go down to the Jerusalem Y and try this in the shallow end of the pool first? We can practice and then walk on the sea in a strong wind." You can't really walk on water with one foot in the boat and one on the sea. It takes all of you. Like Texas Hold'em, it's an "all in." You cannot "kind of" walk on water. You can't "kind of" be a Christian.

    d. Peter might want to wait until the sea settles down. Do this a little later when the wind isn't blowing and the waves aren't so high. We might want to put off following Jesus until our life situations are all in line. It rarely works that way. When we sense Jesus calling, it's "go time."

        Again, you may want to share what your hesitancies were in giving your life to Jesus and how you see them today.

7. Peter steps out of the boat and walks on water. Wow! Then what happens? He messes up. Maybe he thinks he's doing this on his own; maybe he gets anxious and worry overwhelms him in the torrent of the sea (life) and he turns away from Jesus; maybe he starts missing his friends and bailing water (his old life). He is scared and prays possibly the quickest prayer of all time,

"Lord, save me," as his body sinks in the sea. (How long does it take for the water to move from his feet to his head as he sinks? Is it like dropping the ski rope and slowly sinking? Or is it only a second?) Again, it is the honest cry of his heart. What is Jesus' reaction when we mess up? Does He turn away, disappointed, frustrated, or angry at us? Also, when in trouble, Peter didn't turn back to the boat for them to help, nor did he try to swim on his own strength; rather he turned to Jesus for help.

As my three sons first began to walk, my wife and I would position ourselves only three feet from each other. You know the scene. We would hold out our arms and say, "C'mon, you can do it." Each son took that first step and crashed and burned on his first try. At this point, did I stand up, kick them, and say, "You stupid kid. What kind of son are you ever going to be? You can't even walk. Good grief." And then walk away? Of course not, I'd reach down, pick them up, dust them off, and say, "It's okay, my man. Great effort. Let's try it again."

Jesus immediately, immediately, **immediately** reached out, grabbed Peter's hand, pulled him up, and probably with a loving chuckle said, "You lost your faith, didn't you? Why did you doubt me?" Implied in His own words were, "I will always be there — keep coming — we'll make it together — you can count on me."

You may have examples from your life of "messing up" after "giving your life to Jesus." When you share your "failings," focus on Jesus' reaction to you, your healing and redemption, not your "mess up."

Rich, Young Ruler

Luke 18:18-27; Matthew 19:16-29;
Mark 10:17-27

Background

1. In Israel in Jesus' day, the classes of people were clearly defined. There were the wealthy (or the ruling class) and the common people (by far the largest group), whom we might call "blue collar" today: artisans, farmers, shepherds, and others. There were also the religious professionals (the Levites), who included scribes, Pharisees, Sadducees, and temple workers. (For an explanation of the different Levites, see #10 Background, Point 2.)

2. How do we know that this man was rich and young and a ruler? From Matthew 19:20 we see "young" referring to this man. From Luke 18:18, we see he was a ruler. And, from Luke 18:23/Matthew 19:22/Mark 10:22, we see he was rich. Consider this: psychiatrists tell us that there are four external factors that can shape a person's self-image and view of life. They are wealth,

power/position, good looks, and talent/abilities/intelligence. This man had all of these. We can assume by being young and having access to the best of care, his looks were more than acceptable; and he would have had every resource available to him to develop his mind and skills. Yet, he senses something missing as he (like all of us) pursues happiness and life to the full.

3. The disciples lived in a world when wealth was considered a measurement of God's blessing. "If rich people couldn't be a part of God's Kingdom, then who could?" they thought. Jesus answers what we know — that we can't force our way into a relationship with Jesus by trying harder, nor can we get others to "change their heart"; it's humanly impossible. Only God does it.

4. There have been many theories put forth about the expression "a camel through the eye of a needle." One is that this refers to a ship's cable. Another is that it is the name of a gate that, as it is lowered, some will try to enter quickly through a shrinking opening. All these explanations point to something that is difficult but not impossible. However, these theories have little historical merit, and the accepted explanation is just what it says. Getting a camel through the eye of a needle is impossible, but it is a funny picture to imagine. Jesus was often comical and playful, if you'll look for it.

Setting

Jesus is traveling around the region of Judea beyond the Jordan (Mark 10:1 — look at a map if interested) when approached by this rich, young ruler asking a significant question.

Points You Could Make

1. Mark 10:17 — Picture it: the rich ruler must be accustomed to people coming and possibly bowing before him. Here he goes out, finds Jesus and kneels before Him. Wow. Notice, most people bowed before Jesus — the leper, Satan (in a demon-possessed person — Legion, Luke 8), a synagogue ruler, and more. What does this say about Jesus' persona, the One who was fully God and fully man?

2. Matthew 19:16 — His question: "What must I **do** to **obtain** eternal life? Remember he's kneeling as you imagine the tone of his voice … pleading and desperate. He's been searching for a while, seeking out the teachers, philosophers, soothsayers, maybe even the palm readers and fortune tellers. He says, "Good teacher," to which Jesus answers and seems to say, "Do you realize how you've addressed Me? As good? Only one is good — God. Himself. That's right, you've addressed Me correctly. You've searched everywhere for the answer to whole life, and now you've come to the One who created it. Are you ready, for here comes your final, definitive answer?"

He's asking about "eternal life". (For an explanation of the word life — "zoë" — see #3 Abundant Life.) The adjective in Greek here is "aionis," which we translate as "eternal." We incorrectly think eternal refers only to the concept of life from now to eternity. "Aionis" refers instead to a quality or a character of life — a fullness, a depth, a goodness, a richness, which does include life everlasting; however, eternal does not mean only life forever. This man knows there is much more to life/to happiness than wealth, position, power, intelligence, talent, and looks. He's asking the Inventor of Life, "What must I do to have completeness, wholeness, fullness in life?" A great question for all of us. Like our Declaration of Independence says, we all are on the search for "life, liberty and the pursuit of happiness." What can we give ourselves to in hopes of obtaining this eternal life? Maybe here you could talk about what you gave yourself to in hopes of "obtaining" whole LIFE?

3. Luke 18:20, Matthew 19:17 — What's strange about Jesus' answer, "Keep these commandments?" It's the wrong answer. Jesus is setting him up for the right answer. Certainly, living true to God's law (the 10 commandments), especially the "relational" commandments (which Jesus mentions here), is a good thing. If everyone did, life would be better. But remember, Christianity is not about our effort to live well to get close to God or to earn God's favor. Rather, it is about a love affair with God, where through friendship with Him, He and His Spirit live in us (at our invitation) and imparts **Abundant Life** to us. It's about trusting our hearts to Him as Lord, and receiving (not **do** to **obtain**) His love and His life.

4. Luke 18:21, Matthew 19:20 — The man's answer is not arrogant and filled with pride — "I've kept all these since my youth"; rather, it's a desperate cry — "I've tried doing these things, and I know there's more to it." Or, "I can't be good enough." He says, "What am I lacking?" He seems to be saying, "I've given myself to lots of life strategies, including this one you suggest, and I'm still empty, falling short. Something is missing; I know that. Help me, please." We often come to God with a performance mentality.

5. Mark 10:21 — Here is that word "sphlochna" again. (For an explanation, see #2 – Point 4 and #5 – Point 1) What Jesus tells the man next, He tells him in love.

6. Mark 10:21 — Jesus doesn't pull any punches here. As He sees deeply into the man, He knows that he is attached to his wealth in a way that robs him of life itself. Jesus is not telling all of us to go sell everything we have in order to truly experience abundant life. Jesus has identified for **this man** what he is giving himself to in hopes it will bring him life. For each of us, we are giving ourselves to something or someone in hopes of life … a sport, a relationship, pleasing someone, money, possessions, drugs, a group of friends, all kinds of things. Jesus is saying, "Attach to Me; be freed from those things; I'll give you life." Again, share personally from your own life.

7. Mark 10:22 — Jesus didn't run after him, put His arm around him and say, "C'mon … give a little here … sell a few things and see how it feels. We can work this out." Jesus says, "I want all of you." And, Jesus deeply respects us and protects our choice. Though His heart breaks over some of our choices, He lets us walk away.

8. Mark 10:23-27 — Jesus has an interesting conversation with His inner circle, the 12 disciples, about the power that wealth wields with a person. We must treat this point with great care, choosing our words carefully, or we can teach the point Jesus makes incorrectly. See I Timothy 6:10 where the Scripture says that it isn't money that is evil, but the love of money, meaning our attachment to money, which can hold us captive and rob us of life. This ending conversation that Jesus has with His disciples reinforces that God calls and changes hearts. We didn't figure out God, choose God, accept God on our own wisdom or strength; it is a gift **from** God. With us — impossible; with God — all things are possible.

Turning Footbath into Vintage Wine
John 2:1-11

Background

1. There were six stone water jars, holding up to 30 gallons each. These were for the guests to wash and clean themselves before entering the wedding celebration/ceremony. This cleaning was part religious — for purification or becoming clean, and part practical — for washing the dust and grime from their bodies, especially their feet (remember, sandals and no asphalt roads). The Scripture tells us they were partially full having been used for this cleaning. Jesus says fill them to the brim. He doesn't say, "First wash the pots out; remove all the dirt residue from the day's cleanings." He just said fill them to the brim. Have you ever mopped a floor? Then, you've seen how the water turns dirty as you rinse the mop (in this case possibly a towel or sponge) for the next application. So, 30 gallons in six stone pots equals 180 gallons. That would be 908 bottles of wine.

2. John 2:11 — Says this was the first of Jesus' "signs." There are seven such signs in the Gospel of John, meaning miracles revealing Jesus' glory as **the** Son of God and the Messiah, which point to the supernatural power of God giving us His grace as He makes a way for us to be close to Him.

3. Cana was not a wealthy city; it was more poor/rural. Therefore, running out of wine could well have been from lack of money. Marriages in Jesus' day were most often arranged by the families, so probably the young man and woman wouldn't have known each other well prior to this wedding week.

The young bride would have been revealed as from her modest upbringing — a double embarrassment.

Setting

Weddings in Jesus' day lasted about a week, culminating in the actual wedding service followed by an extravagant meal. It was a huge party atmosphere, with wine flowing freely. As the celebration progressed, you could imagine folks grew louder, less inhibited, slurring conversation, dancing more wildly. Jesus, God in the flesh, was right there in the middle of the party. To run out of wine at this point would have been an immeasurable embarrassment to the bride's family. It was not just a breach of etiquette; it was a social catastrophe that would have followed them (never forgotten) for the rest of their lives in that community.

Points You Could Make

1. Your impression of Jesus up to this point might be one who is boring, a killjoy, and a party-pooper. Here we see Jesus was invited and went to parties (these were not tame parties) and His first miracle was to make vintage wine from footbath water to keep a party going. He's not a party-pooper, but a party-maker. He is about festive joy. In Matthew 11:19, Jesus is accused of being a drunkard. Wow! He wasn't drunk. The One who invented life was so full of life that their only explanation for living so freely without inhibition was, "He must be drunk." Jesus a "bore"? Hardly.

2. John 2:4 — In our English it sounds like Jesus talks down to His mother. But, this isn't the case. We can't hear the tone of His voice. "Woman" in Aramaic (the language spoken by Jesus) is a simple and common form of addressing someone; so, He's not being disrespectful here toward His mother. Jesus is hesitant to reveal Himself, saying something like: "Perhaps, you shouldn't involve me. It's not time yet for me to start my public ministry and my steady walk to the cross." In the end, He honors His mother and her request.

3. Imagine the servants doing the most idiotic, absurd thing of all time. They refill footbath jars and take this water to the Master of Ceremonies. What were they thinking and feeling? This is the last day of their jobs, maybe of their lives ... ready in an instant to point their fingers at Jesus, saying, "He said to bring it to you." Why did they even listen to Jesus? What about God-in-the-flesh commanded their attention that they trusted Him? Jesus never said, "Here's what will happen" (He rarely does). He asks for trust. The last verse, verse 11, says the disciples, who knew what happened, believed in Him. Believe in English is the word "pisteuo" in Greek (the language The New Testament is written in). It means more than making an intellectual assent — "I believe." It means you put your life there along with the belief. You don't just say, "I believe that lake is frozen solid enough to hold my weight"; rather, "pisteuo" means you are out there actually walking on the

lake. Your "belief" and your "action" are one and the same. It translates better as **TRUST**. Share any personal experience of listening to God or trusting God (what moved you to do it) without knowing the outcome first — and, of course, share what happened? God is trustworthy.

4. John 2:10 — Jesus made footbath water into wine, vintage wine, and way more wine than the situation called for. God can do that. He can take our messes (even our very lives) and make them better than we can imagine.

Paralytic Through the Roof
Matthew 9:1-7; Mark 2:1-12; Luke 5:17-26

Background

1. Houses were functional only for sleeping in Jesus' day. People cooked and lived outside their houses. Houses were smaller — basically one-room structures made of stone with four walls and few or no windows. There was little wood. Roofs were made of beams, thatching and mud (no shingles back then), which would need to be changed/kept fresh fairly often to maintain its waterproof quality. So, most houses had a stairway to the roof on one side of the house.

2. The religious leaders of that day meant the equivalent of the leading pastors, preachers, denominational officers, seminary professors, and bishops of our day.

   Pharisees: The most influential religious leaders of the Jews. They taught and lived in strict adherence to the law, whether oral tradition or the written law, and explained it precisely. It would be hard to imagine much joy in a Pharisee as they lived to the rules.

   Sadducees: They were more political religious leaders; always wealthy; aristocrats. They held only to the written law, and not to the traditions like the Pharisees. On points of theology, they didn't believe in the resurrection, nor angels or demons.

   Scribes (lawyers): Closely associated with the Pharisees ... they studied and interpreted the Jewish law.

   Sanhedrin: The highest Jewish tribunal, made up of Pharisees, Sadducees, and chief priests.

Setting

What you read is what you get. All the best and brightest of the religious leaders from all over Israel were gathered inside a house in Capernaum listening to the Master "preach the Word to them" (Mark 2:2). Mark says there were more than could fit in the room. Many were outside trying to see or hear, craning through the door.

Points You Could Make

1. Mark 2:3-4 — Imagine the conversation the four friends had in deciding to take him to Jesus, then telling their friend they were taking him to Jesus, and the paralytic's reaction. Imagine the four friends coming up to the gathering, which was spilling outside the door … tapping on the shoulders of folks and reasoning with them to let them in with their paralyzed friend to be healed by Jesus: "Don't you want to see a paralyzed man walk? This won't take long … just let us in, healing happens, and we'll be gone." Their frustration grows as no one budges or gives them any leeway. They're shouting now: "Come on. You're supposed to be the good, religious folks who care for those who are sick. You're the ones who are sick. Have some compassion on us here." Imagine being so focused in on someone teaching, listening so intently, that they give no attention to the folks begging to bring their friend to Jesus. Have you ever been so enthralled by a speaker like that? Folks were riveted to the inventor of life sharing about this life He created. Fascinating.

2. Mark 2:4 — These four are some of the most faithful friends I've ever seen. They are doing whatever it takes to help their friend. A good story here from you about something a friend has done for you that was over and above might make a good introduction to a talk on this event.

3. Mark 2:4 — It says they couldn't get to Jesus "because of the crowd." How does "the crowd" today block our way to Jesus, to even seeing or considering Jesus? Share some examples you've seen or experienced.

4. Mark 2:4 — They go up on the roof and start digging a hole through the thatching and wide enough to lower their paralyzed friend through it. Paint the picture for your listeners. One of the four says, "We've come this far; we're going on the roof. "The others protest, but he convinces them. Maybe the sound of walking on the roof makes everyone look up. Dirt starts falling on the crowd; they start yelling and moving away so they don't get hit. A small opening appears. A head pops through it, and you can hear him say, "This is the spot," and they keep digging. What's the owner of the house screaming? Something about insurance? What is Jesus doing and saying? Maybe nothing? Chaos … now Jesus has stopped teaching and everyone is talking. Hear the tone of their voices? They lower their friend down. I hope he's strapped to the cot or he'd fall off as he can't hold on (paralyzed). Can they lower him down evenly/level? Now, everyone's quiet as this scene unfolds. What will Jesus do or say? Four heads are leaning over the huge hole in the roof. Imagine Jesus and the paralytic's eyes meeting as he's lowered down. Can the paralytic speak? What does he say?

5. Mark 2:5 — Jesus says, "My friend, your sins are forgiven." Now, a loud roar of many voices breaks out. The four friends yell down, "Sins? Heal him for goodness sake. We didn't bring him all this way for his sins." The religious leaders only see that Jesus has made Himself equal to God, as only God can forgive sins. What does the paralytic say? Maybe he's numb/bewildered and can't speak. Maybe he says, "What?" How much time goes by until Jesus speaks again?

    Obviously, the thing keeping the paralytic from experiencing all of life is that he's paralyzed. His biggest problem in life is — he's paralyzed. Is Jesus playing a game here? Or, using him to make some point?

    No, Jesus was addressing his biggest problem in life. In fact, all of us have in common with the paralytic the same biggest problem … sin. (See #6 – Point 5 for an explanation of sin and why it's our biggest problem.) Jesus looked past his disability to his "insides," and he was just as broken there as anyone of us.

6. Mark 2:6-12 — These verses contain remarkable, awe-inducing things about Jesus:

    ➤ He knew what those in the crowd were thinking.

    ➤ He proved His authority as God and over sin by forgiving and healing the paralytic.

    ➤ He addresses heart things and relationship-with-God things (sin); forgives sin as well as physical healing (paralyzed can walk).

    ➤ His "need meter" goes off again as He cared for the wholeness of the paralytic.

    ➤ The people declared in awe, "We've never seen anything like this."

Two Events: The Synagogue Ruler and the Daughter of God

Matthew 9:18-26; Mark 5:21-43; Luke 8:40-56

Background

1. There weren't numerous churches and multiple denominations in Jesus' day. It was the Jewish faith and each town had one synagogue (and there was only one temple, which was in Jerusalem). The synagogue ruler was a very important person in that city — very well-known and very influential. Think of the best-known, most-important person in your town — that was Jairus in this Scripture.

2. See #2 — Background #2 for an explanation on being "unclean" by virtue of this woman's bleeding.

3. In Jesus' day, when someone died the family hired mourners who would stay around and cry, even wail out loud, to have a mood of mourning the death.

4. See #4 — Point 3 for an explanation of becoming "well," which Jesus declared to this woman.

Setting

A crowd had been waiting for Jesus to arrive. How long had they been waiting? We don't know. But the anticipation and excitement had been building. They were already warmed up, ready for action, maybe even swarming Jesus by the edge of the lake, making it difficult for Him to even walk and enter the town. Everyone wanted His healing touch, or a word from Him about life.

Points You Could Make

1. Mark 5:22-23 — Jairus, the most important person in town, falls at Jesus' feet, pleading, desperate, begging for help. There's nothing like a father's love for a hurting child. (This is true for earthly fathers and for our Heavenly Father when He sees us hurting.) Still, to bow before another man is incredible and speaks of the presence that Jesus (Creator of the universe) must have been. (Of course, all will bow, including you and me one day — Philippians 2:13.)

   Also, both the most important person in the community and a common person (sick for 12 years) believe/know/have a view of Jesus that He could actually help their situations. Do we? What if Jesus was God and He cared — would you turn to Him?

2. Mark 5:22-23 — When Jairus asks for help, can you see Jesus' disciples start whispering to one another, (and maybe saying to Jesus), "Jesus, if Jairus was on our side, in our corner, he could open doors for us and advocate for us. Things would go better and others might think more highly of us if you helped him. I'd go to his house, Jesus." Of course, Jesus is not motivated by this kind of thinking, but by hurt and need, so He goes with Jairus. So does the whole crowd.

3. Mark 5:24ff — Let's think about the woman. What was her illness? We aren't sure. Some sort of internal hemorrhaging — an ulcer or something that was slowly killing her, sapping any energy she could muster. What did she feel (help kids identify with her as they feel many of the same things)? She must be weary, possibly depressed, hopeless, full of despair, desperate, self-esteem eroded, self-confidence gone, identity ruined, lonely and alone, confused, prayed/hoped only to have disappointment after disappointment, resigned to "this is how it is," bleak, and more. Have you felt some of these things?

4. What did she look like? First thoughts are often sunken face, disheveled hair and dress, sneaking up under the cover of the crowd. Or maybe she had makeup on, wore a smile, had her hair combed and was well dressed. In other words, if you saw her that day, you may never have known what was going on inside her. In fact, we all cover up and hide (mask) what is really going on in our lives. You may give examples from your life, or from people/kids you've known, about how we wear masks to hide our very selves from one another and how that robs us of life. We also wear a mask to present to others the image we think they'll accept. This has the same effect.

5. Many of us have "bleeding" on our insides. Not real blood, but wounds to our heart caused by people we cared about or were friends with. Betrayal, abandonment, verbal or emotional abuse or manipulation, an ended relationship, a failed expectation, a death, or something else. At the very least, these arrows to our hearts may cause fear and protection/control at all cost, which hinder our ability to trust, to open up, or to risk. There's much more that could be said here, but from your experience in life, you could make this "internal bleeding" point.

6. She did try all she knew to get better on her own. We, too, try all this world has to offer to make life work, to overcome our bleeding. But, she (and we) needed more.

7. The whole scene of Jesus knowing "power" had gone out of Him and looking for who touched Him is glorious. The disciples' disbelief: "Really, who touched you? Everyone is pressing in and touching you." When she touched Jesus, this made Him "unclean," but instead of uncleanness flowing from her to Him, healing and cleanness flowed from Him to her. This is how it goes in a relationship with Jesus.

8. Mark 5:33 — Here is the double or triple miracle: Jesus heals her; her bleeding stopped. It says that she told Jesus the "whole truth," or "her whole story." Imagine, Jesus listened to her whole story. Do you think she started when she first noticed her bleeding? Yes. Then, did she walk through all 12 years of suffering? Yes. How long did this take? Fifteen minutes or more? A crowd around with their own needs, and Jairus waiting with a dead daughter, and Jesus takes 15 minutes with her. Yes. She had no name. In fact, in our Bibles she is called in subtitles "The Hemorrhaging Woman." Jairus has a name; she doesn't. Jesus then names her in verse 34. He calls her "my daughter." It's the only time in the Gospels that we have record of Jesus calling someone, "my daughter." What did listening to her story and calling her "my daughter" do for restoring her self-image, her worth, and her identity … a total healing?

9. We have record in the Gospels of Jesus raising three people from death to life (there most certainly were more). This young girl, Lazarus in John

chapter 11, and the widow's son from Nain in Luke chapter 5. Raising someone from death to life has to rank right up there in miracles "proving" Jesus to be God. Jesus once said, "If you don't believe my words, then look at my works, they bear witness as to who I am" (John 10:37-38). The hired mourners laugh at Jesus as He enters the house. I wonder how many laugh at Him when He leaves the house?

10. Jesus' words to Jairus when He receives word that his daughter has died: "Don't be afraid … only believe."

First — Don't let fear overwhelm you. Fear of what? The truth your daughter could be gone and imagining all that comes with that truth. You get paralyzed and see things skewed and make bad decisions when fear dominates.

Second — "only believe." The Greek word used for believe is "*pisteuo*." It means more than intellectual assent. If you say, "I believe the lake is frozen thick enough to hold me if I walk on it," "*pisteuo*" is you actually walking on it. The action follows the mind's belief. It is better translated, "trust." This is a question in life: Who or what are you going to trust? You can run with that in your talk, if it fits.

Clearing/Cleansing the Temple

Matthew 21:12-13; Mark 11:15-19
Luke 19:45-48; John 2:13-17

Background

1. Jesus' clearing or cleansing the temple is one of only three events in Jesus' life (other than the cross and the resurrection) that appears in all four Gospels. The other two? The woman anointing Jesus' feet (#15) and the feeding of the 5,000 (#5).

2. In Jesus' day, we must understand that the idea of the pilgrimage to Jerusalem was fundamental for every family. Jerusalem, THE CITY of God, contained THE TEMPLE, the place where God dwelled (in the Holy of Holies, a room inside the temple); it was a spiritual home to everyone. To go there for any festival/feast was wonderful and planned for (like we do a family vacation or spring break), but to go for Passover was the height of spiritual experiences. When you went to Jerusalem, you would want to offer a sacrifice to God to cover (or atone for) your sin. So, in John 2:13, we find men selling animals and exchanging money in the temple area. Traveling too far to bring their own animal, they would have to buy it there at the temple, and to buy it they needed to have their money exchanged into temple money. Also, they needed temple money to pay a temple tax. The money changers and animal sellers both charged exorbitant rates, a double-whammy.

3. It would be difficult to explain all about the Jewish sacrificial system in place (from the O.T. law, particularly Leviticus) to atone for your sin. Sacrifices you could offer for your sin ranged from pigeons and doves to cattle. All the poorer people could afford would be a small bird, which still took a lot of their money. They paid the cost gladly to be able to offer a sacrifice.

Setting

1. Matthew, Mark and Luke place this event right after Jesus entered Jerusalem riding on a donkey (Messiah prophecy fulfilled from Zechariah 9:9) to the people's cheering, waving of branches, and laying down their coats in front of Him; so it was at the end of Jesus' three years of His ministry on earth, the week prior to His death. John, who records signs revealing the Messiah has come, speaks of this event right away in chapter two of his Gospel. John also gives more explanation of the event, so this usually is the main text to use for this talk.

2. The Gospels set the scene well. Jesus walks into the Temple and observes the commercialization of selling animals for sacrifice (from doves to lambs and cattle) and the extortion of money changers because you had to have "temple money." And observing this, Jesus "goes off."

Points You Could Make

1. This may be the most dramatic scene picturing Jesus other than the horror of the cross. It blows away any primary image we've carried tending toward a meek and mild Jesus carrying a sheep around on His shoulders. John 2:15 tells us He made a whip, weaving cords of rope together. Jesus must be seething. Anger building up ready to explode. I wonder how long it took to look around and find some rope, and then to make His whip, all the while thinking about what this temple court had become. Then, the Scripture says Jesus "drove them ALL out of the temple." Livestock in panic, feeding on each other's fears, evolving into a stampede, people screaming and getting out of the way like the Bull Run on the streets of Spain, corral fences being smashed down — pure chaos.

    Then, Jesus overturned the money changers' tables, with coins and money flying everywhere. The people working in the temple aren't weak folk who just get out of the way. They are cursing Jesus. They are calling for the police and dialing 911. They are rushing Him to restrain Him.

    What is Jesus saying? Is He yelling cattle drive sounds? Is He permitting the money changers to gather their money before driving them out? Luke and

Mark record Jesus yelling some words from the Old Testament we'll look at in a moment. The noise is wild. The Scripture indicates only one person, Jesus, is making all this happen. This is the same Jesus who heals a leper or tenderly healed and restored a bleeding woman. What does Jesus reveal about God's heart in the temple clearing?

2. Mark and Luke have Jesus saying, "My house shall be a house of prayer and you have made it a robber's den" (quoting Isaiah 56:7 and Jeremiah 7:11 from the Old Testament), and John has Jesus saying, "Zeal for my Father's house will consume me" (quoting Psalm 69:9). Jesus is plenty mad, raging anger, and incredibly passionate here. Why? God wants people to know Him. God wants people to enjoy Him and the life He created. God wants us to connect with Him. The Jewish leaders (see #10 Background for an explanation of the Jewish leaders) had hindered people in coming to God, creating more burdens for people rather than freedom and extorting money from people in God's name. This infuriated Jesus; it makes us angry too. Other times we see God's heart revealed in Jesus' anger when He speaks harsh words to the Pharisees in Luke 13:10-17, Matthew 12:34, Matthew 15:7-9, Matthew 23:13-35, and John 8:44-45. Jesus abhors fake religion for show and barriers that keep people from Him and life. Again, burdens, obstacles and fear were being laid on people instead of grace, pathways to connect with God, and joy in worship of Him. God hates injustice in the world and religion that makes being with God confusing or difficult.

Possibly you could relate an experience you've had that distorted the grace of having a relationship with God and how you've experienced Jesus differently now.

3. Note Jesus' remarkable blend of power and gentleness. He could wield a whip or go toe-to-toe with a Roman emperor, and the next moment touch the sores of a leper or take up a child in His lap.

Lifting Up Jesus

The Woman at the Well

Found only in John 4:1-45

Background

Read John 4:9.

1. There existed between Samaritans and Jews a racism that might even run deeper than any experience of racism in our country (USA) — and we, of course, have racism. It wasn't just that they didn't associate with one another (which they didn't), or that the Jews thought they were better than Samaritans (which they did think). Each had disdain for the other — actual hatred. They would be "OK" if something happened to the other, or if the other were simply not around anymore. How does "classism" come to be when they are both Jews and they both worship the same God, Yahweh? How do they come about in the world today? (You could relay a quick story of an experience you've had with extreme prejudice.)

   One way this enmity between Samaritans and Jews worked out was during travel. To go from Judea or Jerusalem to the Sea of Galilee, the shortest route was through Samaria, but Jews wouldn't dare travel this way. Instead, they'd go down to Jericho and over to Galilee, going around Samaria. This added many miles to the trip and extended the travel time by two days; yet, they didn't think twice about this.

   If you want to read more about how the enmity began and grew between the Jews and the Samaritans, read II Kings 17:24-41 when strangers and Jews came back into Israel and mixed cultures.

   Also note that Jesus lifted up and honored Samaritans from this event in John 4 and the Good Samaritan parable in Luke 10. Also, the leper who turned back to say thank you in Luke 17 was a Samaritan.

2. Women in Jesus' day (and to a large extent still today in the Middle East) had a low position in the culture. They were not to go to school or express ideas. They existed to prepare food, keep the house, procreate, and that's about it.

   One woman's job in keeping house was going to the well to draw water and bring it back to the home. They would typically go early in the morning and late in the day to avoid the blazing heat in the middle of the day. They would all go together. You can imagine the conversations among them (or should we say, gossip among them).

3. So, Jesus crosses a racial barrier, a cultural barrier, a gender barrier, and a moral barrier to engage with this person. That's our God.

4. John 4:5-6 and 12 mentions that this very well was Jacob's well. This is from the Old Testament; if you want to read about its origin, read Genesis 33:18-22, Genesis 48:22 and Joshua 24:32.

5. John 4:6 — The day starts at 6 a.m., so the sixth hour was noon.

6. Living water in the Bible (and here) often refers to the Holy Spirit … Jesus' giving of His Spirit. We will not make a distinction here between Jesus and His Spirit, but rather will speak of the benefits of having Jesus and His Spirit live in us — of abundant life.

Setting

Jesus and His disciples chose to travel the shortest, most direct route to Galilee from Jerusalem, which takes them through Samaria. The disciples leave Jesus alone to rest at the well while they go into the nearest town for some food (see John 4:5-6, 8).

Note: You cannot read this whole event out loud in your talk; it's simply too long. You will need to choose some verses to actually read and some parts to narrate. You will also need to break up the event into "chunks" to use at a time, probably not using the whole event (45 verses).

Points You Could Make

1. This woman came at noon (v. 6) by herself. This isn't the typical time. We hear just a snippet of her pain-filled life in verses 16-18. Perhaps, she has no friends, disgraced in the town. She comes alone, apparently an outsider to the other women.

    Draw kids in helping them connect with this woman's pain from broken relationships, trying hard to have friends and intimacy (give love and be loved), her loneliness, her wanting to be part of a group but left out, her shame, her failures, her feeling far from God, her life not going the way she'd like yet can't do a "do-over," and more. Perhaps, you have a point of contact with her story you could tell from your own story.

2. Jesus goes through Samaria where no Jew goes. Jesus, a Jew, talks to a Samaritan. Jesus treats a woman with respect. Jesus isn't "put off" by a broken, sin-filled life, but enters in. Jesus offers living water/LIFE to one that the culture marginalizes and classifies as the "least likely." In all this, Jesus reveals our God whom we cannot see (John 1:18). We have a God who gains our respect and is trustworthy. This is a God I want to get to know. We have a God who would relate to one such as me. There is nothing you can do or have done that would keep Jesus away from you. He reaches out to us precious image — bearers whom He created. This woman, nor we, need to pass a spiritual SAT test to get in. Jesus doesn't straighten her out or chastise her life choices at first. In the same way, we don't get our act together to get God; rather, we get God and He helps us get our acts together! We never see Jesus having compassion on someone because they deserved it, but rather, because they were in need.

3. Jesus begins by asking her to give Him a drink. (John 4:7). The Greek (original language of the Bible) construction of this sentence shows it isn't a command like: "Give Me a drink now"; rather, it's a polite petition like: "Please, could you get me a drink?" Of course, Jesus could have gotten Himself the water, but what a beautiful, disarming way to begin with the hurting woman. He puts Himself in a lesser, dependent, asking position. God does this! In His pursuit of us, He doesn't play His God card at first.

4a. Jesus does not shame her for her life choices so far. He doesn't give her a sermon or exhort her to make some changes in her life. Rather, Jesus receives her and points her to something better in life.

4b. Verses 10 and 13-14 — This is the big point: Jesus offers us living water, a wellspring inside of us bubbling up to eternal life (for an explanation of life, "zoë," see #3). Living water ... water is essential to life, even more than food ... no more thirst ... the ultimate water. So, the reference is where are we looking for life; where are we looking for our insides to be made whole and right; how are we moving toward healing our broken hearts, finding our significance, and being comfortable (even excited) about our passions and self-image? We all are going to attempt to quench our thirsts — the question is: "What well are we going to?"

5. Always bring out the wonder of Jesus from these events. Jesus was fatigued, (really, He was exhausted) showing He was human (we often forget that He was fully human). Jesus is the great "barrier breaker" as He crossed every forbidden social barrier. In John 4:10, Jesus says, "If you would only **ask** ... He would **give** ... ." The word give is "*dorean*" meaning **free gift**. Jesus freely gives, mirroring Isaiah 55:1ff. In John 4:15, the woman answers (or asks) a bit flippantly and obviously not totally understanding (like us often), yet Jesus still responds favorably, freely giving.

6. John 4:26 — Jesus clearly reveals Himself ... He always does. He will to us also.

7. John 4:28-30 — The woman "left her water pot ... ." When people see what Jesus is about, and taste life with Him, they often leave the old life behind. And people notice the change pretty quickly. Living water on our insides is like that.

The Woman Caught in Adultery

Found only in John 8:1-11

Background

1. John 8:5 — "The law" and "Moses commanded us" refers to more than the Ten Commandments. It refers to the rules for living given by God for the

Hebrew nation (the Israelites, the Jews, God's chosen people) contained in the Torah, the first five books of the Bible. The law also revealed the character of God to the people (before Jesus came and revealed God and His heart). Yes, these Scriptures did command the death of adulterers in Leviticus 20:10 and in Deuteronomy 22:22-24. This shows how serious God took the marriage covenant between two people, which is for our good. One could make the argument that this capital punishment in that day was a deterrent to violating the sanctity of marriage.

Setting

John 8:2 — This verse sets our scene. It was customary for a rabbi to sit while teaching (see Luke 5:3) and people would sit "at their feet" to learn. This event takes place in the temple (and not in just some town), which heightens the intensity to the highest level possible.

1. Imagine this scene. It is R-rated, maybe X-rated. These unkind men set up a woman and grab her while "caught in the very act." Do you think they said, "Hurry up and get dressed; we have somewhere to be?" No. Do you think she had the quick reaction to snatch the bed sheets to half cover herself, or is she naked there in front of the crowd? Do you see her weeping, hunched over in a ball, covering herself there in the dirt and gravel? Do you think they kindly set her down or were more like policemen who throw someone down face-first to handcuff the person to make the arrest, pushing him or her into the back seat of the police car?

   Where's the man? The law says he is equally as guilty. What cruelty with no regard for this woman. Think of her shame, thrown down "in the middle of the assembly," humiliated beyond belief.

   Imagine their tone of voice as they say to Jesus, "The law says … . What do you say?"

   The entire focus for the deeply religious (Pharisees) was "to nail" Jesus publicly. For them, the end justified the means.

2. The Pharisees (for more on the Pharisees see #10, Point 2) were extremely jealous of Jesus. The people were flocking to Him and His teachings of grace, truth, life, God, and His kingdom living. As they felt threatened in losing their place and position of importance, wealth, and authority, they made plans to discredit Jesus and later to dispose of Him by whatever means needed. This is the first of their many entrapments. Ingeniously planned, it seemed fail-proof. They know Jesus favors grace and mercy and even forgives sin; so as He sets this adulterous woman free, the Pharisees can claim Jesus has come to undo or rewrite the law, which would destroy Jesus' reputation as rabbi or as God Himself. If Jesus allows this woman to be stoned to death for her sin, then His grace message and new kingdom-living teachings are invalidated.

Lifting Up Jesus

Points You Could Make

1. You can see a wonderful window here into God's heart. Jesus is primarily concerned with this frightened, shamed woman, even before what could happen to Him in this trap. This is really unfathomable to us, as any of our minds would be racing as to how to respond to defend ourselves; self-preservation would win in our hearts. But not God's heart. Our care is His primary concern.

2. John 8:6 and 8 — Why does Jesus stoop down and write something on the ground with His finger? (and, what does He write?) Some speculate that He was buying time to think of His response. Others say that He was writing down the names of all the accusers in the crowd. But, the answer that makes the best sense is that every eye would have craned to see what Jesus was writing, and therefore, attention was diverted from all eyes on this woman.

3. Jesus addresses her kindly and tenderly (hear His tone of voice — is it accusing or condemning or disappointed?) starting with "woman." This was a normal greeting in that day — friendly, showing respect. It's how Jesus addressed His own mother in John 2:4 at the wedding at Cana. He doesn't say, "C'mon honey, you know better"; or, "What are you doing with your life?" followed by a lecture on right and wrong. He asks a disarming question, "Did no one condemn you?" followed by, "Neither do I." Wow! Again, Jesus takes us as we are — messed up, broken and sin-filled — and offers us a life with Him.

4. We also see Jesus is not light and easy on sin. It breaks His heart (Genesis 6:5-6) and robs us of life (Psalm 32:3-4).

    a. John 8:7 — By asking those without sin to throw the first stone and no one then throwing even a single one, you could weave into your talk that of course, none of us are without sin (and what that means). For more explanation about sin see #10 and #6). Certainly, the older you are the more honest you become about yourself and your motives, your life's choices and their consequences; so it makes perfect sense that the older ones dropped their stones first.

    b. John 8:11 — Jesus tells the woman "to leave your life of sin." He doesn't ignore her sin. He doesn't acquit her without question. Instead, while not condemning her, He asks (not commands) her to give up the way she's been living (that is less of life anyway), and live a new way (preferably with God at the center).

    c. The dropping of the stones was the result of a movement in the heart known as "conviction." It is more than feeling guilty for doing something wrong; it is the Spirit's convincing in our hearts before God and His way. What we see here as conviction is explained in John 16:8-11.

    d. How did this woman feel about herself? About the way God treated her?

Lifting Up Jesus

About God? About how she will now choose to live? We don't live for God in order to gain His favor or qualify for something from Him; rather (as in this encounter), we experience God — His love, kindness, favor, and blessing — and we respond by living with Him and for Him.

15 Woman Anointing Jesus
Matthew 26:6-13; Mark 14:3-9
Luke 7:36-50; John 12:1-8

Background

1. This event is one of three events that appears in all four Gospels (besides the trial, cross and resurrection of Jesus). That alone makes this event significant. In addition, at the end of Matthew and Mark's account, Jesus says, "Wherever the Gospel (the Good News of my love for you and of my rescue of you) is preached in the whole world, tell this woman's story." Jesus elevates what this woman has done to a whole new level.

2. Mark 14:5 — "Three hundred denarii" — A denarius was considered a day's wage; three hundred denarii was then the equivalent to one year's wages (300 working days in a year). Think of a bottle of perfume worth one year's wages (the median wage in the U.S. in 2010 was $45,000) poured out over Jesus' head and feet. Scholars believe Mary was formerly a prostitute prior to meeting Jesus; thus the comment by the dinner host in Luke 7:39, "If this man were a prophet, He would know who and what sort of person this woman is who is touching Him, that she is a sinner." A prostitute with a wealthy clientele might have a $45,000 jar of perfume.

3. This event took place in Bethany, a town near Jerusalem where Jesus would retreat after a day's ministry in Jerusalem. He was usually at the home of Lazarus, whom He raised from the dead — the home of Lazarus' sisters, Martha and Mary (Luke 10:38-42 and John 11:1-46).

Setting

1. Matthew, Mark and Luke's account set this dinner at the home of the Pharisee named Simon, now called "Simon the Leper." Most assuredly he was no longer a leper or he would not be hosting a dinner. He must have been healed by Jesus (perhaps Mark 1:40-45) and in appreciation prepared this banquet for Jesus and His entourage.

2. Then the interruption came with this woman's display. Imagine the fragrance of the perfume overwhelming any of the meal's smells. All conversation must have stopped as the people watched (for how long ... 10, 15, 20 minutes?)

this woman pour the perfume on Jesus' head (Matthew and Mark) and over His feet (Luke and John), weeping and wiping His feet with her hair, all the while kissing them, over and over. See Simon ... outraged at this intrusion into his home that disrupted his dinner party ... He's got to be yelling. Hear the disciples' judgmental and condemning tone of voice as they "indignantly" (Webster defines this as "an expression of anger or scorn at something unworthy, improper, or below one's position.") rebuke the woman directly or speak about her to each other ("Why this waste?"). Observe Jesus ... calm and quiet, glowing/radiating with appreciation in being honored, concerned for the woman's well-being and for her reputation with this crowd, maybe even pondering/daydreaming about His imminent death ("She's preparing my body for burial," Matthew 26:12, Mark 14:8.). Paint the scene as you imagine it.

Points You Could Make

1. What is your answer for the reason Jesus is so delighted by this woman and her action toward Him? Why does He lift her up higher than anyone else's belief, trust or faith in Him? Above the prophetess Anna, who worshipped and waited at the temple for Jesus for over 50 years (Luke 2:36-38). Or more than the woman who believed that if she only touched Jesus' garment she would be healed. She touched it and she was healed (Matthew 9:20-22). Or, above the soldier who told Jesus that He did not even need to come to his house, but simply say the word and his servant would be healed. Jesus did heal the soldier's servant from afar, enabled in part by the soldier's faith (Matthew 8:5-10).

   Was it her worship, her adoration of Jesus"? Was it her "total focus" on Jesus, not caring about what others thought? Was it her anointing His body for His upcoming burial? All these could be true, but I'd offer that for Jesus she was a snapshot of what He had been trying to communicate during His three years of ministry. Jesus was essentially saying, "My Gospel is that I love you, regardless of who you are, where you've been, or what you've done. Will you let me love you? If you receive/accept my love into your inner being, I will heal you of any brokenness and free you of anything that holds you prisoner. This woman "gets" me. She's received my love and is simply loving back. You tell her story." The first "rule" of having a relationship with Jesus is, "Let yourself be loved by Him."

2. Matthew 26:8 — "Why this waste?" We all are somewhat (or a lot) controlled by what others think of us. We will say things or do things that aren't really who we are, just so others will think well of us. The disciples scolded her (Mark 14:5) and spoke indignantly about her/to her (Mark 14:4). We fear that if we follow Jesus, we'll be viewed as she was viewed (and, if we are honest, we think this was a waste). Our crazy world with its priorities and pecking orders has made what is good and normal (following Jesus, being loved by

Jesus) seem weird and abnormal. She "gets" life to the full, but even the disciples think she's "off-line."

3. Once we've tasted Christ's love for us, nothing else satisfies or fulfills us. Yet, this woman represents a fear that we have of growing closer to Jesus. That is, we will change into a "Jesus freak." This woman appears to be groveling, crying and weak. She was an object of scorn in the eyes of those other people. She looked foolish in front of others. You may think, "No thank you, that's not for me." But before you write her off, look more deeply at her. She's been loved at her most inner place by our God, accepted, her sin forgiven, and has been given an eternity of oneness with Him. We all deeply need and long for the same. Doesn't she have the true freedom that seems so elusive for us? She does not care what others think of her. She is not performing for Jesus, trying to get Him to respond in a certain way, or to earn His approval. She has peace for the first time in her life. She knows she's loved by God Himself. Here you could share how God's love for you has changed your life — how you've experienced peace and freedom.

4. Mark 14:8 — "She has done what she could." What a beautiful, encouraging sentence this is. Jesus marvels and celebrates our effort — any effort — toward Him or His work. We don't have to worry about: "Am I doing this correctly?" "Is this enough?" or "Is this what I should be doing?" Jesus affirms that we should "do what we can" and He receives it. This relationship with Jesus isn't something we need to master or totally understand before we jump in and let Him love us. Share an example from your life of "doing what you could," and your experience of Jesus in it.

Jesus Calms a Storm
Matthew 8:18, 23-27; Mark 4:35-41; Luke 8:22-25

Background
1. For an explanation of the Sea of Galilee, see #5 – Background and #6.
2. For an explanation of the storms on the Sea of Galilee, see #7 – Background.

Setting
This event's "set-up" is obvious. Jesus often retreats from the crowds by getting in a boat when he needed rhythm in his life. As you "paint the picture," you may include any boating stories from your life (mine has seasickness involved☺).

Points You Could Make
1. If (or when) we question Jesus' humanity, or struggle to imagine Him as a

person, this event helps. He was totally exhausted, falling into a deep sleep, even though a storm is rocking the boat.

2. If we're honest, this may be our fear about God: He created everything and threw it into motion, but He's asleep when we're in a storm. He's distant and we feel abandoned in our time of need. This sentiment might be best captured in Mark 4:38 where they scream at Him desperately (can you hear their tone of voice?), "Don't you care?" They (like we) ask the One who even gave His life for our well-being (see Isaiah 53:4 and Romans 8:32) if He cares for us. If Jesus quit caring for us, He'd cease being God.

3. The big point is, of course, that storms come upon us as we live life. Every one of us has a personal story of a storm and how Jesus helped us through it — often with surprises — not the way we would have expected and not in the timing we had hoped for. The last line from each Gospel account of this event is glorious: "Who is this, that even the wind and waves obey Him?" This Scripture opens for you the opportunity to unwrap the answer to that question. It is THE question you want kids to ask: Not just "who is this man ... ," but also who is Jesus to me/for me?

4. The disciples "go" to Jesus for help in the midst of the storm. They were afraid. They had probably tried to bail water and row like crazy. They had most likely exhausted their own ideas. They didn't go to Him with heroic faith, calm and knowing He could help. But they did turn to Jesus and He helped. "Who do you turn to in the storms of your life?" This is a question you could ask in your talk.

Bartimaeus Regains His Sight

Luke 18:35-43; Mark 10:46-52
Other similar miracles of Jesus helping the blind to see
Matthew 20:29-34; John 9 (whole chapter)

Background

1. There were no special considerations for the blind in Jesus' day — no handicapped parking place, no braille in the elevator, no trained seeing-eye dogs, no special typewriters or schools for the blind. It was quite the opposite. You were left to fend for yourself, beg for food and money, and were viewed as cursed or out of favor with God ... you were blind as the consequence of some sin in your life. The question in John 9:1-2 portrays this prevailing thought of that day (the thought that God punishes humans for sin is still around today though). The blind beggar was often strategically placed at the city gate for the best exposure to the most "traffic" (of people) in order to do well in receiving gifts (see Luke 18:35, Matthew 20:29 and Mark 10:46).

2. It was a sign that Messiah had come (God had visited His people) when the blind began receiving their sight (See Luke 4:18, Matthew 11:2-6).

Setting

Imagine Bartimaeus and paint the picture bringing the Scripture to life. How is he dressed? Unkempt, unshaven, stuck in the dust, certainly not clean (maybe smells of B.O., stale urine, or alcohol). We'd compare him to one we call "homeless" or a "street person" today. No one cares for him. No one pays him the time of day. Where does he sleep? Where does he go at the end of the day and how does he get there? He is marginalized, discarded, and considered worthless by society. Help the kids to relate to Bartimaeus or identify with him. The Scripture tells us he once could see and lost his sight (Luke 18:41). Imagine that! He knew a life with sight, but circumstances changed and he was helpless to change them back. How does he feel about God? That God took his life away, and he was blind because of God? "How could He be a good God or a God who cares? Look at me, obviously He doesn't care about me." How does Bartimaeus feel about himself? Low self-worth, helpless and hopeless? Kids can relate to a lot of that. Tie in, if appropriate, how you identify with Bartimaeus, how you've experienced despair.

(In Matthew 20, it is two blind men ... Can you imagine their conversation before they call out to Jesus? "Should we call out? Is He the One? What will happen to us? Will He stop? Let's do it!")

Points You Could Make

1. Luke 10:36; Matthew 20-29, 31 — "A great multitude" was following Jesus. There was always a multitude wanting to be near Jesus. Why? To see a miracle? Sure, but it was more than that. He had the words of life; never had they heard someone teach/speak like Him — true, right, helpful, accurate, and full of grace. Imagine God sharing about the life He created, knowing everyone (seeing into them) like He did. He exuded the abundant life He spoke of ... joy, peace, wholeness, genuineness, and more radiated from His person. People felt (knew they were) loved by Him. See Matthew 20:34 — here's that word "*sphlochna*" again (read #2 – Point 4, and #5 – Point 1 for the explanation of "*sphlochna*"). Bartimaeus could sense it: Jesus, God in the flesh, stopped and gave His full attention to one deemed unworthy. Most people love because something/someone is worthy to be loved; Jesus' love makes someone worthy ... His love brings worth to the one loved.

2. Jesus' question is profound: "What do you want me to do for you?" If we stop and think, "Is the God of the universe really asking me — little ol' me — one of six billion people on this planet, what do I want God to do for me?" Does He care? Yes, He does. This is a great question to get kids talking about life, their longings and hopes. What would they answer if Jesus asked them this question? Kids might first talk about "circumstances of life" things, but soon move more to deeper, life longings. However, we must use caution that we don't reinforce the common thought that God will hear us and come through for us the way we expect Him to, all the time or every time. We must be careful not to set kids up (and set God up) for failure and disappointment.

3. A blind man's cloak was like a security blanket to him. It kept him warm in the winter and it shielded him from the sun in the summer. Under it, he kept what few belongings he might have held. For Bartimaeus to "fling his cloak aside" as he came to Jesus was significant. Maybe he heard (his sense of hearing and discerning would have been keener, to help compensate for lack of sight) about Jesus and was ready to come toward Him with nothing holding him back. What do we cling to as security or life that might get in the way of coming to Jesus as He calls us? You could identify those things like possessions, position, being known, friends, being liked, attitudes, even bitterness, wounds, shame, etc., which might hold us back.

4. Jesus says, "Your faith has made you well" (Luke 18:42/Mark 10:42). What faith? How much faith? We tend to think you've got to be Billy Graham or the like to be considered a person of faith. Faith is your view of God/ Jesus/His Spirit and your trust and dependence on life with Him. Jesus will take you where you are, even be so pleased with your "tiny grain of sand" faith in Him and be so pleased you had hope and some degree of favor toward Him. Bartimaeus cried out, screaming for mercy at the top of his lungs (and mercy from God isn't a bad prayer to scream). He had the courage to keep pursuing God even when "the crowd" told him sternly to shut-up. Remember, a beggar needs the crowd to like him so they'll give money to him, so he was taking a big step out there toward Jesus. The faith Jesus affirmed in Bartimaeus was not a seminary degree or a lifetime of good works. It was a little courage and a little hope in Jesus. This is an encouragement to us.

5. What would you imagine Bartimaeus' reaction to Jesus would be after receiving his sight back? Jesus didn't demand a response. Jesus didn't say, "Live this way." Bartimaeus doesn't know much about Jesus and what his life will be like with Him. Luke 18:43 — Bartimaeus began following Jesus ... that's what we do too ... giving all that we know of ourselves to all that we know of Jesus — then the relationship grows.

6. Luke 18:42 — Jesus says, "**Receive** your sight." No performance needed. No deserving or earning. No achieving. This is the only world religion where we receive God and His love and action on our behalf. All the others — the Jewish code of law, the Muslim five tenants, the Buddhist path to higher consciousness, the Hindu doctrine of Karma — are all about achieving God's favor. The huge contrast is that we simply "receive" Jesus.

7. As Baritimaeus receives his sight, obviously his life will never be the same. Not only does he see again, but his life as he knew it — begging and being

seen as worthless — is over. All is new. You could talk about how your life changes when you receive Jesus ... the past is gone; all is new ... share how life has changed for you. (II Corinthians 5:17)

18 Lazarus is Raised from the Dead
John 11:1-46

This event (like when we speak of the Samaritan woman of John 4, the blind man of John 9, Jesus and His cross, and some others) is one where we cannot read (or probably use) the whole event involving Lazarus. Kids will get lost if we read all 46 verses, or minds will wander. See below in "Points You Could Make" for a possible breakdown of bite-size verse sections as you bring the Lazarus event to life.

Background

1. Jesus must have visited the home of Mary and Martha (sisters) and Lazarus quite often. We know of the meal and interaction in Luke 10:38-42, and of Jesus spending nights in Bethany at their home during Passover Week (Matthew 21:17) after He spent the days in Jerusalem (see John 11:18). Also, from John 11:2 we learn that it was Mary who anointed Jesus feet (see #15).

2. The prevalent teaching of Jesus' day was that for three days one's soul lingered with the body. Then on day four, it left permanently. This adds to the confusion and hurt that Mary and Martha were feeling over Jesus' delay in coming when they sent for Him (see John 11:17).

Setting

John 10:40-42 tells us that Jesus is teaching and ministering in a place beyond the Jordan when He receives news that Lazarus is deathly sick in Bethany. He then comes after Lazarus dies.

Points You Could Make

1. John 11:1-7

   a. When Mary and Martha sent word to Jesus, the word was only, "The one whom you love is sick." They didn't demand He come, or even ask for an outcome. They just laid before Jesus their situation. They knew Jesus loved them, cared for them, and would respond, so they didn't have to ask for their way. Of course, any prayer is good prayer, but this isn't a bad way to pray.

   b. The minute Jesus heard it, it was clear He had "the BIG PICTURE" in mind. He's God after all. Because Jesus is God (today, too), He knew the case of Lazarus' sickness and death would show the glory of God (see Isaiah 55:8-9). John 11:5 tells us Jesus loved (in imperfect tense meaning it is ongoing/continued loving) Martha, Mary and Lazarus. Then John 11:6 tells us Jesus didn't respond immediately. We often assume God doesn't care if Jesus delays in working our bad situation out immediately; or, that Jesus' "non-action" means He hasn't heard us or isn't engaged with us. These would be wrong assumptions. Through verses 14-15, we are reminded that Jesus is in charge and always up to something. From our earthly viewpoint and human eyes, we don't see it every time.

2. John 11:17-27 — In this dialogue between Jesus and Martha, Jesus declares that He is "the resurrection and the life" and what that means to us. For an example of "the life" Jesus is, see #3; for an explanation of the word "believe," see #9 – Point 3. This is a statement of who Jesus is — that He is greater than death and He offers life, now and always.

3. John 11:28 — Jesus is calling for Mary. Mary is broken and hurting … Jesus knows that (a sparrow does not fall to the ground without His knowing — Matthew 10:29) and calls for her.

4. John 11:32-37 — Jesus wept (John 11:35). The God of the universe has a heart, and it gets hurt. He feels. This is unbelievably significant. Why does Jesus cry? John 11:36 tells us that in His love for Mary, Martha and Lazarus, He wept with them as they hurt. When we hurt, Jesus isn't distanced from us or our pain. He enters in and bears with us. As the old Negro spiritual says, "Nobody knows the trouble I've seen; Nobody knows like Jesus." (See Psalm 56:8)

   A probable reason Jesus cries is that inside He feels the brokenness and pain of the world. Maybe He's feeling, "This isn't the way I intended the world to be. Death wasn't a part. Hurt and pain wasn't a part. I long to bring Real Life, if you'd believe in me." This fits with another time Jesus was moved to tears: Luke 13:34-35.

   Let's say you made up a story about a divine figure come to earth in disguise as a human being. He goes to a funeral of a dear friend, knowing He's going to raise his dead friend to life, making all the mourner's tears turn to joy. Wouldn't you picture him smiling, excited, and confident, maybe even playful? He might say proudly, "Wait until you see what I'm going to do!" How can you imagine this all-powerful, sovereign, divine figure being so caring and vulnerable so as to join in Mary's agony and weep with her? That's our God's heart. (Taken from Tim Keller)

5. John 11:38-45 — The dramatic scene of Jesus raising Lazarus is self-explanatory.

a. Verses 41-42 — Jesus wanted us to know that His Father sent Him; that He came from His Father. We see this over and over.

b. Verse 44 — With the stone removed and Lazarus shuffling out — "mummified" — in grave clothes, we hear Jesus say, "Unbind him." (This must have been much like the banned Saran Wrap Young Life skit. He can't move and could fall flat on his face, unable to catch himself). Doesn't Jesus bring us from death (Ephesians 2:4) to life (II Corinthians 5:17)? He wants us to live free, not all bound up. You could share a way (or ways) you were/are bound, and how Jesus and His Spirit have been helping you become unbound (from things like wounds to our hearts, lies we've believed, shame we've carried, feelings of being unlovable or unworthy, fears which control us, anxiety robbing us of joy, other things).

Notes: